SOCIOECONOMIC DEVELOPMENT *of a* NATION *and* INDIVIDUAL EMPOWERMENT

NEW INSPIRATION OF CREATIVE FORCES

YEAR 2025

DR. ABOUBACAR SIDY SOW PH.D.

Socioeconomic Development of a Nation and
Individual Empowerment
Copyright © 2024 by Dr. Aboubacar Sidy Sow PH.D.

All rights reserved. No part of this publication may be
reproduced, distributed, or transmitted in any form or
by any means, including photocopying, recording, or
other electronic or mechanical methods, without the prior
written permission of the author, except in the case of
brief quotations embodied in critical reviews and certain
other non-commercial uses permitted by copyright law.

ISBN
978-1-962868-67-9 (Paperback)
978-1-962868-68-6 (eBook)

This book is dedicated to my family,
parents, friends, *and teachers.*

———————

*I hope that after reading this book,
scientists, philosopher, and theologians will speak the same
language and will begin to understand one another.*

Dr Aboubacar Sidy Sow Ph. D.

———————

JUST ONE LAW EXPLAINS *THIS WORLD:*

THE *TRIAD'S LAW.*

TABLE OF CONTENTS

Welcome To The Discovery Of The Triad Law Or Triad..... ix
Introduction xiii

Chapter 1	The Triad Law In General 1	
	1.1 Study Of Life 1	
	1.2 Freedom And Happiness....................... 6	
	The first definition of freedom 7	
	The second definition of freedom 8	
	The third definition of freedom 9	
	1.3 Astrological Signs Of Planets 12	
	1.4 Order Of Succession Of Numbers, Days Planets And States Of Soul...................15	
	1.5 Spiral Of Life 16	
	1.6 Stairs Of Life 17	
	1.7 Life Of Beings In General.................... 19	
Chapter 2	Application of The Triad's Law To A Person And Couple of People.............21	
	2.1 Triad's Law Applied To A Person 22	
	2.2 Description Of The Ten States Of Soul Of A Person... 26	
	2.3 Application Of The Triad Law To A Couple Of People 32	
	2.4 Description Of The Ten (10) Types Of Relationships Between Two People..... 35	
	2.5 Conclusion... 36	

Chapter 3	The Triad Law Applied To The Evolution of A Nation 38
	3.1 Description Of The Ten Types Of Societies 39
	3.2 Dynamic Of The Group Of The Negative 57
	3.3 Conclusion 64
Chapter 4	Evolution of Humanity 67
	4.1 Description Of The 7 Phases Of The Evolution Of Humanity 68
	4.2 Conclusion 72
Chapter 5	Signs of Zodiac: 74
	5.1 Period Of Influence Of Signs 75
	5.2 Description Of The Twelve Signs 76
Chapter 6	The Creation 86
	4.1 Interpretation Of The Two First Chapters Of Genesis By The Triad 86
	The First Day 86
	The Second Day 88
	The third day 89
	The Fourth Day 90
	The Fifth Day 92
	The Sixth Day 93
	God's Rest (Seventh Day) 95
Chapter 7	Application of The Triad Law To The Chemical Elements 97
Chapter 8	Significance Of The Ten Universal Numbers 100
Chapter 9	The Great Star Of Life 107
Chapter 10	Hermes' Vision 114

Bibliographie 121

WELCOME TO THE DISCOVERY OF THE TRIAD LAW OR TRIAD

TRIAD MEANS THREE (3) PARTS

One of the biggest problems of our time resides in the fact that science and religion appear as two enemy forces. Each of us carries in himself these two forces that are in appearance irreconcilable. This false disparity between science and religion exists because we are not yet able to find a universal law that could be their common ground. We seem to be aware of the existence of this law in some life scenarios, but in other areas we just fully ignore it.

In his main books: The mystery of conscience and the power of the negative (Year 2001), Socioeconomic Development of a Nation and Individual Empowerment (Year 2018),

Dr. Aboubacar Sidy Sow uses the new definitions of some basic concepts such as life, conscience, soul, and freedom to discover the fundamental law that governs any evolution.

The first goal of this work is to enunciate and develop the structure of this law called triad law or triad. The triad law considers that any being is the combination of three parts. These parts are intention, knowledge, and resource. This being may be mineral, vegetable, animal, or human. It can be as small as an atom, or as big as our univers.

The second goal of this work is to prove the existence and the smooth working of this law in all beings in their static and dynamic forms. At this level, the author uses the wisdom of the philosopher Hermes, the religious Moses, and the scientist Mendeleev to show that these great people have already succeeded in enunciating the smooth working of this law in different life sphere.

The third goal of this work is to use this law for learning how to lead a positive evolution in comprehending some secrets of any life, and foreseeing the future. Using this law, Dr. Sow succeeded to show the present and the alternative futures of our World, the significance of the ten universal numbers, the secrets of the zodiac signs and the secrets of individual, social and humanitarian lives.

This work targets all groups of the society: politicians, scientists, seekers, theologians, philosophers and layman.

It shows to the layman his state of soul, the state of soul of others, and the state of soul of his society. It suggests to him the path he should follow to avoid to be in the negative (subordination, depravation or revolt), and to make a positive evolution toward the next phase.

This work is oriented toward people and politicians of developing countries because we must recognize that most of them are in the three phases of the negative. These phases are the dictatorship system, the corrupt system, and war. This work shows them the state of the soul of their society, the possible evolutionary tendencies, and the right way to follow to leave the negative.

This work is also addressed to the people and politicians of countries who have just succeeded in overcoming the negative but are not yet very advanced in their positive evolution. In this case, there is sometimes a threat of return to the negative.

This group is formed of economically weak countries where there is no longer dictatorship, war, and where the corruption is effectively under control. It enables these politicians and people not only to end with the negative and its tendencies, but also it stimulates them to pursue their evolution toward the next positive phase.

This work orients the politicians and people of advanced countries in their positive evolution. It allows them to be situated in their positive evolution and to identify the others in order to cooperate better.

This work aims at the scientists, and seekers of any domain of life. It gives them the secrets of any classification and evolution since those people meet often the numbers 3, 6, 7, 8, and 10 when talking about groups, phases, periods, domains, dimensions or regions.

This work is addressed to philosophers and religious leaders simultaneously to prove to them, they just are two components of the same entity.

This work calls philosophers to wean of ideology and invites them to reinvest in their mission that is the research of the truth and not the defense of interests.

In other words, this work is important to all people who wish to comprehend this New World explanation in triad's law basics.

INTRODUCTION

After having observed the existence of some real problems in our present world such as:

The complete divorce between science and Religion,
The hijacking of philosophy by Ideology,
The cold war (capitalism vs. socialism struggles of the past decades),

I decided to develop a new philosophical method that I named TRIAD LAW or TRIAD. This new approach is based on logical and mathematical reasoning. It is also free of any ideological tint. The Triad Law gives us the deep secrets to any positive personal evolution and shows us the path to the proper development of nations.

This book has three goals:

Its first goal is to enunciate and develop the structure of triad law (or TRIAD). The triad law considers that any being is made of three parts. These parts are the intention, the knowledge and the resource. The being may be mineral, vegetable, animal, or human. It can be as small as an atom, or as big as our universe.

Its second goal is to prove the existence and the smooth working of this law in all living beings, both in their static and dynamic forms. At this level, I used the wisdom of the philosopher Hermes, the religious Moses, and the scientist Mendeleev to show that these great people have already succeeded in enunciating the smooth working of this law in different life spheres.

The final goal of the book is to use this law in learning how to lead a positive evolution in comprehending secrets of life, and foreseeing the future.

We know that the philosophers of previous centuries divided being into two parts (Matter and consciousness) while the Triad divides consciousness into two additional parts which are the Intention and the Knowledge. The triad goes further and divides the intention into two other parts which are the desire and the Will.

The will is an energy that the being deploys to realize or prevent the realization of a desire. This energy can vibrate positively (in harmony) or negatively (in disharmony) with the heart if the being is a human. The positive and negative combinations of these three components (Intention, Knowledge and Resource) lead the being to seven (7) positive States of soul or to one negative situation. This negative situation divides itself into three states. Therefore, we end up with a total of ten (10) States of Soul.

This Triad law shows us the existing link between the ten states of soul and the ten universal numbers. The seven positive stages of the Triad law may be found through the seven (7) colors of the rainbow, the seven notes of the scale, the seven groups and the seven periods of chemical elements, the seven heavens, the seven days of a week, the seven states of soul etc. It also manifests itself in the constitution of a human, which is triple in essence, but sevenfold in its positive evolution.

This book is addressed to politicians, scientists, theologians, philosophers and ordinary citizens who may wish to understand the proper approach to unlocking the secrets of any life and evolution (as explained by triad's law).

Dr A Sow

CHAPTER 1

The Triad Law In General

Life is action, Being has a triple nature,
Soul is energy

1.1 Study Of Life

Now let's do a detailed study of life based on these three ascertainments.

First: Any being lives as long as he is acting and reacting. As soon as the being stops acting and reacting, he stops living. With this, we conclude that life is action and/or reaction.

Secondly, under normal conditions, any living being's action aims toward getting more happiness and sometimes more freedom; therefore, we can say that the obtainment of happiness and sometimes freedom remains the goal of any life.

Finally, consider any living being. There are other beings living within him/her, and acting and following their own intentions for the obtainment of their own freedom and happiness. These other beings may act in harmony or in disharmony with the individual.

The actions of the other beings living within the host that are in harmony with the host will be called positive actions. The actions that are in disharmony or in discordance are negative actions.

In summary here are these three ascertainments.

1. Any being lives as long as he is acting and reacting.
2. The obtainment of happiness and freedom remains the goal of any life.
3. Positive = Harmony and Negative = Disharmony.

To further understand a being's life, we should study his/her actions in their different phases of evolution in time and space.

So what is an action?

Before acting, the being feels deep within him a need which pushes him to want and desire. A DESIRE is born within him. This desire is always POSITIVE because it vibrates in harmony with your HEART when it comes to you, for example. For you, this desire is positive. Then you deploy an internal ENERGY that we call WILL to support or block this desire.

Let's call Will or Willpower (the energy, courage and perseverance) that you deploy to amplify or cancel a desire.

Your INTENTION (I) is made up of your desire and your Will taken together. Your Intention is said to be POSITIVE when your Will is deployed to ACCOMPANY (support) your desire. Your intention is said to be NEGATIVE when your Will is deployed to BLOCK (prevent) your desire. Remember that your Will is the energy you use to accomplish or cancel your desire.

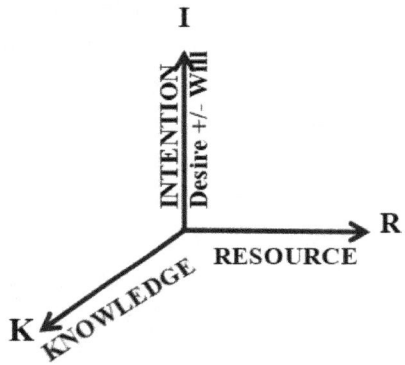

To achieve your desire, you use your information, experience and knowledge. This is what we call KNOWLEDGE (K). When you are acting, you use the material and financial means that you draw from your own body and the surrounding environment. The set of all these elements is called RESOURCE (R). Every being therefore has (3) three one-dimensional components which are: Intention, Knowledge and Resource. When we describe a person in a religious view point, these three components are respectively SOUL, SPIRIT and BODY.

Intention is expressed through the will deployed to act in order to obtain positive results. It is linked to the heart and soul.

Knowledge is affirmed by the technical and technological stock used to act. It is linked to the mind or spirit.

A person's primary asset remains his physical strength, therefore his physical body; the remaining is composed of his material and financial wealth coming from nature and the environment.

In the formulation of his Intention, a person obeys his heart and his emotions. He listens to his heart and soul. Then, he consults his mind (Knowledge). To decide and realize his desire, he listens simultaneously to the heart and the mind. Therefore, he consults his CONSCIENCE (C). Remember that the prefix Con in Latin means "With". So the word Conscience or consciousness means WITH SCIENCE or knowledge. The same composition of consciousness exists in Russian language. In Russian, Conscience means So-Znaniye. The prefix SO means WITH and ZNANIYE means Knowledge. From here follows the definition of consciousness which is an Intention lead with knowledge. Conscience or Consciousness is the domain existing between Intention and Knowledge.

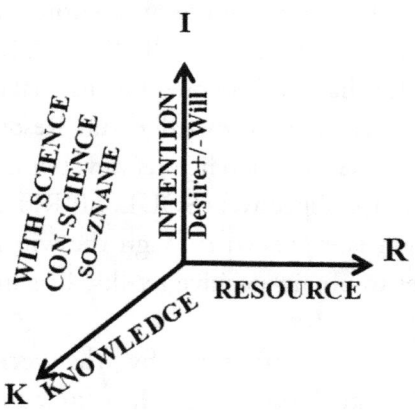

It is also possible that a person acts on his assets without consulting his knowledge; we say that he acts WITH PASSION (emotion). From here, derive the word con-passion or compassion. COMPASSION is an activity (act, agitation) carried out without consulting knowledge.

ACTIVITY (A) is the domain existing between Intention and Resource. That is a process of active transformation of the nature you make to create the material conditions necessary to improve your existence. Activity means emotional action.

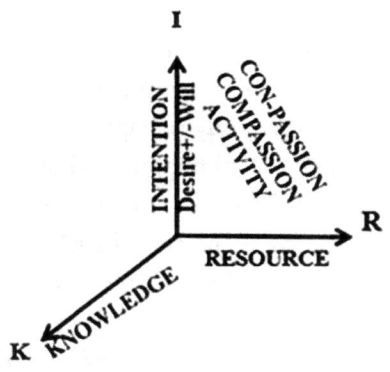

Let us add that POWER (P) is composed of Knowledge and Resource. It is the domain existing between Knowledge and Resource.

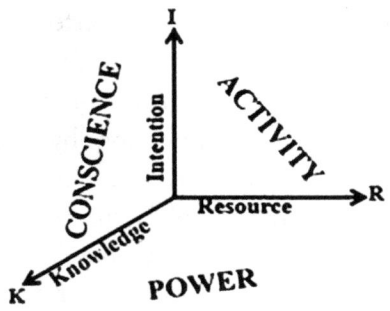

Your power is the combination of your resource and knowledge. It is the set of your technical and scientific experiences, your physical, material, and financial resources. You can buy or sell goods and services to improve your power. For this reason, the money factor plays an important role in the determination of your power.

1.2 Freedom And Happiness

As we stated in the second observation, the pursuit of happiness and sometimes freedom remains the goal of life. In this case, we say that you are happy when you feel that all the three components of happiness that are (Intention, Knowledge and Resource) are positive and in harmony. HAPPINESS remains a sensation, FEELING and even a dream or sometimes an illusion when it does not work in the real world..

We say that you are free when your happiness is accepted by the society (environment) in which you live.

FREEDOM is a collective, SOCIAL concept while HAPPINESS is a PERSONAL concept since the concepts of good and bad, big and small, depend on you only.

Effectively all definitions of the concept of freedom turn around the description of a perfect harmony that should exist between its components. (Power and intention, activity and knowledge, conscience and resource).

If we represent the intention by the symbol I, knowledge by the symbol K, the resource by symbol R, the power by the symbol P, the conscience by the symbol C, the activity by the symbol A, the freedom by the symbol F. And more specifically, if we represent the positive intention by I+, or just I, the negative intention by I- and so on, we will comprehend the three definitions of the concept of freedom.

Let's see these definitions under all three plans.

In each of them, we will quote a philosopher who already succeeded to define freedom under the same plan. All these definitions of freedom are correct depending on the angle of approach.

THE FIRST DEFINITION OF FREEDOM

It's the description of the harmony between your power and your intention.

You are free when you can do what you want.

$$F^+ = P^+ + I^+$$

Let's quote the philosopher John Lock, (1691).

"And consequently the freedom is not an idea that belongs to the volition or to the preference that our spirit gives to an action rather than to another. <u>But to a being that has the power to act or to prevent himself to act according that his spirit will decide to the one or the other of these 2 parts.</u> Our idea of freedom spreads itself as far as this power, but it does not go beyond. Since each time that some obstacle stops this power to act or not act or that some force comes to destroy the indifference of this power, there is no longer freedom and the notion we have of freedom disappears immediately."

Essay concerning the human being intendment triad, L Coste II, chp 20, 1972, p145

THE SECOND DEFINITION OF FREEDOM

It's the description of a harmony between your knowledge and activity. $F^+ = A^+ + K^+$

You are free when you know how to act.

Let's quote F. Engels (1878)

"Freedom is not in the dreamed independence toward the nature law, but in the knowledge of these laws and in the given opportunity to use them rationally in order to reach the goals. This is true for the external nature laws as well as the psychical and physical laws that govern a being's life."

Anti Duhring trad bohigelli, ed soudes 1963 p 146.

THE THIRD DEFINITION OF FREEDOM

It's the description of a harmony between your conscience and your resource. $F^+ = C^+ + R^+$

You are free when your conscience is in harmony with your resource.

Let's quote Henri BERGSON 1889

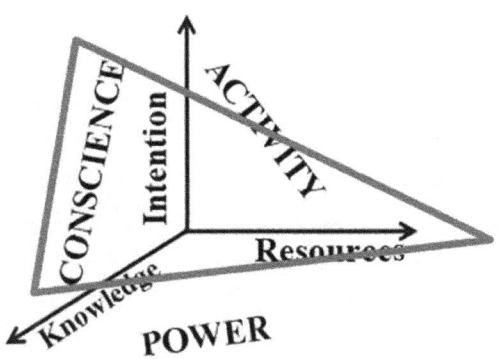

"The act is free when it expresses our complete individuality. We are free when our acts come from our complete individuality, when they have the resemblance that we can find sometimes between the design and the artist.

In vain one can say then we give up to the all-powerful influence of our character. My character is "I" again and because we like to separate a being in two <u>parts in order to consider by abstraction the "I" that feels or thinks and the "I" that acts.</u> It will be childish to conclude that one of these two "I" weighs more than other. If we call free any act that comes to us, the act that carries the brand of our individuality is inevitably free because only this "I" can claim the paternity."

Essay on the immediate data of conscience Chap 3, puf 1967 pp 129

Life is a combination of multiple actions. Conquest of more happiness and freedom is the goal of any action that you freely undertake. So you partially or totally put the three components of freedom expecting a given result. At the end of one or many actions you can see the components of your freedom changing positively or negatively. (Positive, means in harmony with your heart and Negative, means in disharmony with your heart).

At the end of the execution, you compare the actual results to those theoretically expected or forecasted.

It's the psychological impact of the difference between the forecasted and the obtained results that put your soul into a state of satisfaction, deception, neutrality or happiness etc. This is what we call the STATE OF YOUR SOUL or state of your mind.

Instead of you, it could be a group of people, or even a whole society. In the comparison stage, you will appreciate your results from norms and concepts that are proper to you and not necessarily from those commonly adopted. Your norms can be identical or opposite to those commonly adopted. It's up to you to form the concepts of good, bad, evil, big, or small depending on your conscience level.

Plato 368 BC said; "Each of us is judge of what it seems good, and what it is convenient to him."

Baruch Spinoza in1675 added:

"I call good what I desire."

By representing these three components with their positive and negative signs in the same system of perpendicular coordinates, we will obtain a system of eight blocks or 8 spheres or eight cases.

These eight cases can be as follows in taking into account their positive and negative components:

1. $I^+ R^- K^- = I^+ + (R^- + K^-) = I^+ + P^- = I^+ P^- = I\ P^-$
   Case of the positive intention& negative power.
2. $I^+ R^+ K^- = (I^+ + R^+) + K^- = A^+ + K^- = A^+ K^- = A\ K^-$
   Case of the positive activity& negative knowledge.
3. $I^+ R^+ K^- = (I^+ + R^+) + K^- = A^+ + K^- = K^+ A^- = K\ A^-$
   Case of the positive knowledge& negative activity.
4. $I^- R^+ K^+ = I^- + (R^+ + K^+) = P^+ + I^- = P^+ I^- = P\ I^-$
   Case of the positive power& negative intention.
5. $I^- R^+ K^- = (I^- + K^-) + R^+ = C^- + R^+ = R^+ C^- = R\ C^-$
   Case of the positive resource& negative conscience.
6. $I^+ R^- K^+ = (I^+ + K^+) + R^- = C^+ + R^- = C^+ R^- = C\ R^-$
   Case of the positive conscience& negative resource.
7. $P\ I = A\ K = R\ C$
   Case of freedom& happiness.
8. $P^- I^- = A^- K^- = C^- R^-$
   It's the case where intention, knowledge and resource are all negative.

   This one can carry your soul to three different states.

   For this reason, we have eight cases with ten states of soul.

Each of these eight cases corresponds to a state of a soul, a level of energy, or a degree of freedom.

1.3 ASTROLOGICAL SIGNS OF PLANETS

In this section, we will show the existence of a relation or correspondence between planet' signs and states of the soul. To each positive planet and the sun correspond a day of the week and a universal number. We will use the rule of succession of the seven (7) days of the week to show the dynamic nature of the states of the soul. It's what we call the order of succession or path to follow to accomplish a positive evolution.

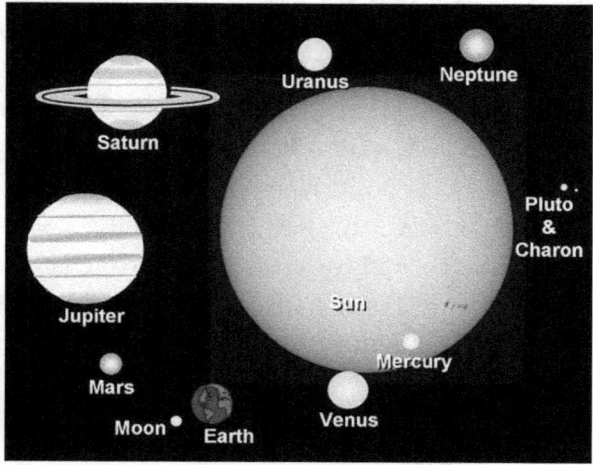

LINKS BETWEEN PLANETS AND STATES OF SOUL

EARTH: Generally in astrology, at the Earth place, one uses its satellite which is the moon. Because of its proximity to the Earth, the moon plays a big role on the emotions of the Earth inhabitants; on their intentions and wills. For these reasons, we can say that the Earth's sign is the positive intention and negative power.

MARS: Named by the Romans, Mars is the god of war, and was also regarded as the protector of the fields; the god of agriculture. They call it the red planet due to its volcanic activity. Its sigis the positive activity and negative knowledge.

MERCURY: In astrology, Mercury is a planet that represents the reason, the communications, and knowledge. They call it the Messenger, the informer. It means that the sign of this planet is the positive knowledge and negative activity.

JUPITER: This planet, because of its large mass, is associated to the expansion and the magnetism. Its actions are considered to be the most beneficial and enlightening for us on Earth, because we are always at the conquest of power. They call it the Giant. The sign of this planet is the positive power and negative intention.

VENUS: In astrology, Venus is associated with all beautiful things: peace, love, harmony, art, and music as well as money and partnership. They call it the Jewel of the Heavens. It means that its sign is the positive resource and negative conscience.

SATURN: Astrologically, it represents the planet of physical limitations. This physical limitation corresponds to the negative possession. Hermes called Saturn the planet of universal wisdom. One calls Saturn the watcher of the threshold. The sign of this planet corresponds to the positive conscience and negative possession.

SUN: The Sun represents your ego and individuality. It shows your ambitions and deepest character traits. It is the life giver, and it represents your vitality and accomplishment. Some solar characteristics are ambition, confidence, strength, leaderships, and desire for recognition. These correspond to your happiness and freedom.

THE TRANSATURNIAN PLANETS

They are Uranus, Neptune, and Pluto. For many astrologers, these planets work on the region of non-conscience. This domain corresponds to the negative. Life is never normal under their influence. These three planets do not tend to wake up our internal potential. When we try to ignore or to reprimand their intentions, they become enemies, and in this case, we submit to them. These planets wake up your degree of spiritual maturity. They are the planets of repression.

NEPTUNE: In astrology, Neptune is the most difficult planet to describe because it rules anything that is difficult to pin down, define clarify in specific terms. Neptune represents the chief of the seas. Neptune is connected to illusions, dreams, and mystical things. They call it the illusionist. The sign of this planet is the submission (seas) and the dictatorship (illusionist).

URANUS: In astrology, Uranus is associated with sudden changes and events for which there is no warning. Sometimes Uranus describes where there is a strong desire to be free or unconventional. It is also associated with rebellious urges. One calls it the awakened because this planet gets us out from the submission by awakening us of dreams and illusions. Its sign corresponds to the false happiness.

PLUTO: The discovery of this planet is linked to the raise of the dictatorship, crime, syndicate and the underworld. In mythology, Pluto was the god of lower region and wielded much power. One calls Pluto the planet of power. In astrology, Pluto is the great transformer. It breaks down the old and replaces it with the new. Pluto is associated with the most drastic changes, forced conditions, mass movements. Its sign is shock, revolt, revolution or degradation.

1.4 Order Of Succession Of Numbers, Days Planets And States Of Soul

To each universal number corresponds a day of a week a planet's sign (name) and a state of the soul.

It's what we call the order of succession.

NUMBER	*DAY*	*PLANET*	*STATE OF SOUL*
1	Monday	Moon-Earth	Positive intention
2	Tuesday	Mars	Positive Activity
3	Wednesday	Mercury	Positive Knowledge
4	Thursday	Jupiter	Positive Power
5	Friday	Venus	Positive Possession
6	Saturday	Saturn	Positive Conscience
7	Sunday	Sun	Accomplishment
8	Night	Neptune	Submission

| 9 | Night | Uranus | Depravation |
| 10 | Night | Pluto | Revolt |

Here is another form of presenting the order of succession.

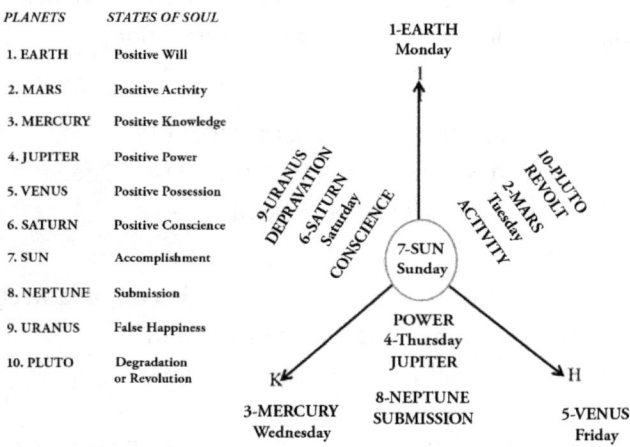

1.5 Spiral Of Life

Finally, we can say that a human's life like any other being's life can be represented as follows.

This is what we call the Spiral of life.

1.6 Stairs Of Life

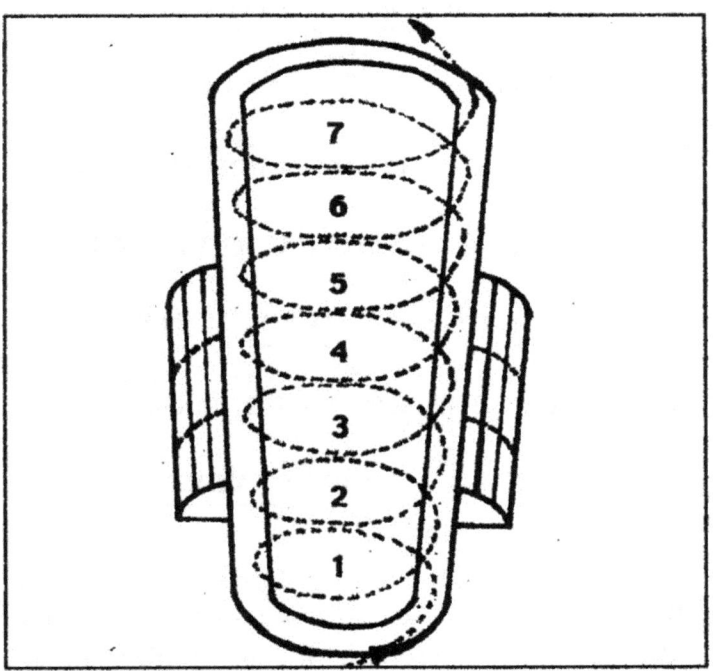

If we cut this spiral vertically, we get what we call the stairs of evolution.

```
┌─────────────────────────────────────────┐
│    STATE OF HAPPINESS & FREEDOM         │
└─────────────────────────────────────────┘
                    ↑
┌─────────────────────────────────────────┐
│     STATE OF POSITIVE CONSCIENCE        │
└─────────────────────────────────────────┘
                    ↑
┌─────────────────────────────────────────┐
│      STATE OF POSITIVE RESOURCE         │
└─────────────────────────────────────────┘
                    ↑
┌─────────────────────────────────────────┐
│       STATE OF POSITIVE POWER           │
└─────────────────────────────────────────┘
                    ↑
┌─────────────────────────────────────────┐
│     STATE OF POSITIVE KNOWLEDGE         │
└─────────────────────────────────────────┘
                    ↑
┌─────────────────────────────────────────┐
│      STATE OF POSITIVE ACTIVITY         │
└─────────────────────────────────────────┘
                    ↑
┌─────────────────────────────────────────┐
│   STATE OF POSITIVE WILL (Intention)    │
└─────────────────────────────────────────┘
                    ↑
┌─────────────────────────────────────────┐
│         BLOCK OF THE NEGATIVE           │
└─────────────────────────────────────────┘
```

This logic works because: It's Monday which produces Tuesday. It's Tuesday which leads to Wednesday. It's Wednesday, which gives birth to Thursday. It's Thursday which introduces and hosts Friday. It's Friday which designs Saturday. It's Saturday that fosters Sunday.

If you look at the positive side from the top to the bottom, you will see that:

Your happiness/freedom depends on your conscience.
Your consciousness derives from your resource.
Your resource stems from your power.
Your power comes from your knowledge.
Your knowledge is from your activity.
Your activity depends on your desire and will.

1.7 Life Of Beings In General

In any life we have the following points.

1. There are 7 successive and progressive phases.
2. Each of these phases is qualitatively superior to the previous phase.
3. The succession of these phases cannot be avoided in the accomplishment of a positive evolution.
4. Each phase can be prepared and determined only by the phase that precedes it directly.
5. If a being does not follow this established order, he/she falls into the negative because he/she will lack the required material or spiritual bases.
6. When in disharmony with the conditions of his environment, a being can easily remain in the negative until his degradation or total demolition, if he refuses to return to the phase corresponding to his level.
7. However, if he realizes soon that he is in the negative, he can return to the phase that corresponds to his level. This return can be done by revolution or by negotiated passage.
8. A being cannot regress without the pressure of an external constraining force. In this condition, he/she will always fight to go to the phase that corresponds to his level. This passage can also be done by revolution or by negotiated passage.
9. So, after several tests of evolution and revolution, the being can arrive to the 7th phase that we call the phase of accomplishment. Once in this

phase the being will feel happy and free. As life is a succession of actions, the being will start a new action again, and so on until he reaches the positive seventh phase of the seventh action. When at this phase, the being will pass to a new structure qualitatively superior.

CHAPTER 2

Application of The Triad's Law To A Person And Couple of People

In the previous chapter, we studied the triad's law in general, in this one, we will apply this law specifically to a person and to a couple of people. This study will allow us to comprehend the different states of soul of a person and a couple of people.

First let's apply this triad law to a person to define the concepts of intention, will, knowledge, resource, conscience, power, activity, freedom and happiness.

Then, with the help of these concepts, we will make a detailed study of person's state of soul.

Finally, we will apply this triad law to a couple of people to bring out the different types of relationship that can exist between two people. This study will help us to understand the origin of the negativity, the causes of its appearance, its expansion and its demolition.

2.1 Triad's Law Applied To A Person

Now, let's apply the triad law to a person and call it an individual triad.

Since a person became the central element of this chapter, we will consider his intention as the referential intention. That referential intention is the one of the person who is acting and using his proper will to reflect, analyze, and decide.

This intention may conform to or oppose judicial, religious, moral, or political norms. It may be liked or disliked by other members of his society. It may be feasible or unattainable. It may be immediate or accomplishable at long term. It may be hidden or not. This is the intention wanted and desired. The most important is that this intention makes his will vibrate in harmony with his heart.

We call this intention a positive intention. Conventionally, we represent it by the letter I^+ or I.

Any intention that is in harmony with this one is called a positive intention. Any intention that is opposed to the positive one is called a negative intention. Conventionally, we will represent it by the letter I^-.

Baruch Spinoza 1675 said: "I call good what I desire."

Plato 368 BC said; "Each of us is judge of what it seems good, and what it is convenient to him."

Let's make a parallel link with the being we studied in the first chapter to define the structure of the triad's law applied specifically to a person.

Before starting let's recall the concepts of positive and negative of certain components.

The knowledge is positive for a person when it is used to accomplish an action judged positive by him, or when this knowledge is sufficiently available to realize an intention judged positive by this person.

The knowledge is negative for a person when it is used for the accomplishment of an action judged negative by this person, or when this knowledge is not sufficiently available to realize an intention judged positive by him, or when this knowledge does not exist at all.

The resource is positive for a person when it is used for the accomplishment of an action judged positive by him, or when this resource is sufficiently available to realize an intention deemed positive by him.

The resource is negative for a person when it is used to accomplish an action judged negative by him, or when this resource is not sufficiently available to realize an intention judged positive by him, or when this resource does not exist at all.

The positive conscience is the combination of the positive intention and positive knowledge.

The negative conscience is the combination of the negative intention and negative knowledge.

The positive activity is the combination of the positive intention and positive resource.

The negative activity is the combination of the negative intention and negative resource.

The positive power is the combination of the positive resource and positive knowledge.

The negative power is the combination of the negative resource and negative knowledge.

The positive freedom or simply freedom expresses a harmony between the positive power and the positive intention. It also expresses a harmony between the positive activity and the positive knowledge. It means a harmony between the positive conscience and the positive resource.

The negative freedom or the negative expresses a harmony between the negative power and the negative intention. It also shows a harmony between the negative activity and the negative knowledge. It means a harmony between the negative conscience and the negative resource.

Having explained once again the concepts of positive and negative of certain components, we now start our study by applying the triad law to a person.

Now let's consider a person acting without any external pressure, using freely his resource and his knowledge. Before acting this person foresees a result for him. After the action, he gets some results that can be the same or different from those he expected.

It's the impact of the difference between the expected and the obtained results that put him to a given psychological state that I called his state of soul.

Since we deal with a system of three perpendicular components: intention, knowledge, resource with their positive and negative signs, we get a total of eight cases or eight situations.

1. Situation where the intention is positive while the power is negative. It's a situation of the positive intention I P^-.

2. Situation where the activity is positive while the knowledge is negative. It's a situation of the positive activity A K⁻.
3. Situation where the knowledge is positive while the activity is negative. It's a situation of the positive knowledge K A⁻.
4. Situation where the power is positive while the intention is negative. It's a situation of the positive power P I⁻.
5. Situation where the resource is positive while the conscience is negative. It's a situation of the positive resource R C⁻.
6. Situation where the conscience is positive while the resource is negative. It's a situation of the positive conscience C R⁻.
7. Situation where the intention, the knowledge and the resource are all positive. It's the positive situation A K, I P, C R.
8. Situation where the intention, the knowledge and the resource are all negative. It's the negative situation C⁻ R⁻, I⁻ P⁻, A⁻ K⁻.

This situation called the negative, leads a person to one of the three negative states of soul. This is why we end up with a total of ten (10) states of soul.

First negative state of soul. A person tries to survive while abstaining from any individual intention, ambition and initiative. He becomes constantly and completely submitted. He puts his will and his power at the disposal of his master. *That is the state of neutrality or submission.*

Second negative state of soul. Being submitted a person decides to be completely but not constantly at the disposal of his master. To get some happiness and to forget its true problems, he creates parallel activities that give him some pleasure. *This is the state of false happiness or depravity.*

Third negative state of soul. This case occurs, when a person decides to find his happiness and freedom by breaking completely and definitively with the submission and depravity. He decides to break all existing structures at any cost including death. *This is the state of revolt, revolution, or degradation and the beginning of a new life.*

Now let's us make a detailed study of these 10 states of soul.

2.2 Description Of The Ten States Of Soul Of A Person

1. State of the positive intention and negative power

You are in this state when you have the will necessary to lead an action you like, but you have no material and financial means, nor the knowledge and techniques necessary to realize it. In this stage, you are limited to the willingness and the gain of resources remains your first goal. You are free to desire, to wish, and to want but all stops there. Your happiness resides in the accumulation of money, material and physical force. This is the case of a newborn baby. Today it is the case of nonqualified human labor forces in developed countries.

2. State of the positive activity and negative knowledge

You are at this stage when you have the intention, the will, and succeed to get material and financial means that you desire in spite of your lack of knowledge and information necessary to lead positively this action. It looks like you are acting and succeeding by chance. This is the case of a young kid growing physically with no knowledge and without technological means. These people are recognized by their great activity followed by a low level of profitability.

3. State of the positive knowledge and negative activity

You are here when you are obliged to sell your will, your physical and financial possessions to get knowledge, new techniques and information. This is the situation when school children and students are obliged to spend their will, time and their money for learning. People in this stage are always looking for new techniques and technology to set or to maintain their leadership over opponents and competitors. It is the case of seekers, businessmen, farmers, entrepreneurs, bankers looking for new techniques in order to set or maintain their leadership over their opponents and competitors.

4. State of the positive power and negative intention

You are in this state when you face an action that you do not like to realize while you have the information, knowledge, techniques, material and financial means necessary to achieve its realization. This is the case of young students after graduation. This is the case of indecisive people who do not like to take actions. This behavior is very frequent with those that are used to execute orders.

5. State of the positive resource and negative conscience

You are in this state when you are obliged to sell your will, knowledge for getting a material and financial dividends necessary for leading positive actions. In some cases you are obliged to do a program that you do not like. This situation happens often to qualified people who receive dividends in form of salary.

6. State of the positive conscience and negative possession

It's when you decide with all your heart and conscience to expend some material and financial means in order to accomplish a not for profit action. You may be in this state when you become wise and decide to make sacrifices. You may also be in this state when you lead some non for profit or charity actions. That is the case of religious, artists, people of culture and those who work with love.

7. State of freedom and happiness

In this stage you have not only the will and the power necessary to realize an action, but you also set and realize your goal. Here your power and will are positive. Your activity and knowledge are positive. Your spiritual side is in harmony with your material side. At this state, you have all human values in place. This category of free and happy people is formed of all persons who generally succeed not only in acquiring a good intellectual education, establish solid social relationships, but also in securing a strong professional career with a good level of income and working with love.

CASE OF THE NEGATIVE

The eighth case, which is the case of the negative, leads to three different states of soul. For these reasons we have eight cases but ten states of soul.

The first way is when the being submits to a dictatorship. *The state of soul that corresponds to this behavior is called neutrality.*

The second way is when the submitted being creates actions that give him a false happiness. *The state of the soul that corresponds to this behavior is called false happiness.*

The third way is when the being decides to separate himself completely and definitely from the dictatorship by using force. *The state of soul that corresponds to this behavior is called revolt or revolution.*

8. The state of submission or neutrality

In this state a person has not courage, nor the knowledge, the financial and material means necessary to accomplish the action he desires. Therefore, this person decides to submit himself to his master. He can no longer act from his own initiative. He uses his physical forces and intellectual power to accomplish the wish of his master. The master can be another person, nature in general, an animal, a political or religious system, a cult etc. This person finds his happiness when he is unconditionally submitted to his boss. The more he is obedient, the more he feels happy. Only the master can give, take care, instruct, protect, punish and give access to his liberty. Today this state of soul exists with people living in the political and religious dictatorships.

This situation of submission occurs also when an educated and rich person is obliged to put his will and his power at the disposal of an authority. A consequent person accepts this life only if he knows that he will be free after some time of subordination. He knows that he is in this condition because he did something wrong to others. To get his freedom he should lead these negative actions for a given time. That is the case of prisoners.

9. State of depravation or false happiness

This state occurs when a submitted person decides to leads parallel actions that give him some happiness but not freedom. In this state, he takes actions that cannot solve his real problems.

These actions are executed to replace the ones that have given him more happiness and freedom.

This person keeps hope believing that he will ultimately get the right to happiness and freedom. Unfortunately, this is only an illusion because his hope will never be realized as long as he will be in the depravation.

Being unable to take positive actions, he will spend part of the time on negative actions and the other in subordinate actions in order to rest and forget his miseries.

With the time, the use of alcohol, drogues, lies, robberies, misappropriation and undisciplined behavior become regular practices.

By losing his hope, he understands that his ambitions will never be realized. He says himself that he either persists in depravity or breaks once for all with this structure through a revolt.

10. State of revolt, suicide or revolution

A person enters into this state when he loses hope in the future of his actions. He understands that if he wants to be master of his actions, he has to absolutely break with his current situation.

Not wanting to live in submission for eternity, or living in depravity and humiliation for limitless time, he decides to use his financial and material means to destabilize the existing structure. He knows that he can only find the path to happiness when he completely destroys the existing structures and builds a new and more equitable life. He can also run away to explore new horizons by exodus or commit suicide.

Generally this state of soul is the one of the unemployed people, workers with very low income, businessmen in bankruptcy, young work force without financial means, people without hope for a bright future. At this stage, any person says himself, either succeed in his action, or go into exile or commit suicide. If he succeeds, the revolt becomes a revolution and he gets closer to the real happiness. If he fails, he departs towards other skies.

Each of us at any time may find himself in one of these ten states of soul.

2.3 Application Of The Triad Law To A Couple Of People

In the first part of this chapter, we studied the person's state of soul. Now we are going to study the types of relationship that can exist between two people. We know that each of these two people has his intention (soul), his knowledge (spirit), and his possession (body).

When these two people are united, each one combines his three components with those of his partner. These components are combined following their nature.

Example: the soul of the first can only be connected to the soul of the second. Therefore, we will see the combination of two souls, two bodies, and two spirits. Each combination can be made in harmony (positively) or in disharmony (negatively).

Let study each case of these possible combinations. First let's define some concepts.

Total harmony

There is total harmony between two beings, when respectively their spirits, their bodies, and their hearts exist in harmony at the same time.

Harmony of the hearts

Two hearts like one another when each of them wants the other to be happy. Each of them feels a sensation of happiness when making the other happy.

Disharmony of the hearts

Two hearts are in disharmony when the happiness of the first does not represent the happiness of the second. Here, these two hearts like opposite things. What one likes is detested by the second

Harmony of the spirits
Two spirits are in harmony when they have similarity in their experiences, reasoning, and knowledge.

Disharmony of the spirits
Two spirits are in disharmony when their experiences and knowledge are different and even their reasoning are different.

Harmony of the bodies
Two bodies are in harmony when each of them finds other attractive. This can be by the physical form, health, age, color, manner of walking, and dressing. In this precise case the money factor can play a very important role since it helps to fixe many defects through cosmetics.

Disharmony of the bodies
Two bodies are in disharmony when they do not have mutual attraction such as physical shape, health, and manner of dressing.

Harmony of the powers
That is a harmony not only by the reasoning capability, but also by the physical body, the financial and material wealth.

Disharmony of the powers

It happens when the power of the first cannot be in harmony whit the power of the other. They cannot complete each other not only in matter of reasoning but also in matter of age, wealth and physical health.

Harmony of the consciences
It happens when there is a harmony in their judging, and decision making. They like similar things and they have the same reasoning. They have in general the same notions of good, bad, small, great, beautiful, etc.

Disharmony of the consciences
This is when two people decide in different even opposite manners. They have opposite notions of good, bad, small, great, beautiful, etc.

Harmony of the activity
This is a harmony in emotions, in passions, in the form of expression and execution of love and pleasures.

Disharmony of the activities
It happens when they are not compatible in matter of pleasure, rejoicing, and sexual life.

Now by applying the triad law to these two people, we will discover the ten types of relationships that can exist between two partners.

2.4 Description Of The Ten (10) Types Of Relationships Between Two People

The first type is when they are in harmony with their hearts and in disharmony with their powers.

The second type is when they are in harmony with their activities and in disharmony with their spirits.

The third type is when they are in harmony with their spirits and in disharmony with their activities.

The fourth type is when they are in harmony with their powers and in disharmony with their hearts.

The fifth type is when they are in harmony with their bodies and in disharmony with their consciences.

The sixth type is when they are in harmony with their consciences and in disharmony with their bodies.

The seventh type is when there is a total harmony. It happens when two partners have in common their hearts, spirits and bodies in harmony. Their spirits are in harmony with their activities. Their consciences are in harmony with their possessions. Their hearts are in harmony with their powers. This is the state of common happiness and true love.

Now when their common happiness is in harmony with the real world, they become happy and free. That is one of the goals of a marriage.

It means, the road leading to a common freedom passes through common love and common happiness.

Total disharmony.

This happens when two partners are in disharmony with the hearts, spirits and bodies. In this case we have three types of relationship.

The eighth type is when they are obliged to be together, and one of them accepts to submit to the other in term of heart, spirit and body.

The ninth type is when they are obliged to be together, and each of them leads his one life in order to find happiness with a third person.

The tenth type is when both decide to no longer be together, and to break definitively the link that unites them. That is the advent of the total separation (Divorce) of two hearts, two spirits, and two bodies.

2.5 Conclusion

Finally we can classify these ten types of relationships in four groups.

The first group is the one of perfect harmony. We will call it group of true love or group of love.

The second group is made of the harmony of the heart or the combination containing a harmony of the hearts like the activity or the conscience. We will call it group of friendship between two people.

The third group is made of the harmony of the spirit, or the power or the body. We call it the group of business relationships.

The fourth group is the combination of the types of relationships where there is a total disharmony. We call it group of the negative love or group of the negative.

Comparing the first and the fourth groups, we will remark that in the first group we have a positive love while in the fourth, we have a negative love.

This negative love exists when there is no love at all. We say in this condition that the love is negative by non-existence.

This could also be when the heart of each person is oriented toward a third person. We say in this condition that the love is negative by opposition.

The negative can exist also when the love exists but in insufficient quality. We say in this condition that the love is negative by insufficiency.

We see that the negative can manifest itself by one of these three conditions (inexistence, opposition or insufficiency).

We can say also that the greater the tension in the negative by opposition, the larger its power. And more the negative becomes powerful and tends to rupture the union.

The power of the negative always depends on this tension. The energy of this tension feeds the negative. We can manage the negative only by acting on the gravity of the tension.

The couple can get out of this negative by setting a business or friendship relationships.

The couple can get out of the negative by definitively and completely breaking all structure of the union. This is a total divorce.

CHAPTER 3

The Triad Law Applied To The Evolution of A Nation

To accomplish a sustainable development, any nation should get out of the negative and go gradually through the seven positive phases of the stairs of evolution. These are the stairs of evolution.

NUMBERS	STATES OF SOUL
1.	Positive Will
2.	Positive Activity
3.	Positive Knowledge
4.	Positive Power
5.	Positive Resource
6.	Positive Conscience
7.	Accomplishment.

When a nation refuses to follow this path, it will fall into the negative.

A nation is in the negative when its population is obliged to do what it does not want.

In this position, we have three different types of behaviors.

First: The people are obliged to accept to submit to dictatorship. This is the state of submission of the people to the dictators.

Second: Being under submission, the people lead a life of depravity or false happiness to forget their problems. This is the state of false happiness or depravity.

Third: The people decide to break with the constraining structure by using force at any cost. This is the state of shock, revolt, revolution or demolition.

It should be noted here that many countries of our world today are in the three phases of the negative (Dictatorships, Corruption or Revolt).

To accomplish a sustainable development, any nation should pass gradually through the seven positive phases of the stairs of evolution.

3.1 Description Of The Ten Types Of Societies

1. Society of Positive Social Will

This is a society where the intention of the leadership is in harmony with the one of the people, but there is a lack of material, financial, technical and intellectual means to execute the intention of the people. This type of society is formed after dictatorship or depravity phases when new leaders arrive in power through democratic institutions. It can also be formed after a revolt, followed by a democratic revolution. That allows the complete destruction of the former system and its replacement with another one where the leaders are elected democratically.

The leaders arrive to power after the organization of transparent, free and democratic elections. Then the justice system begins to become functional and freer. A democratically elected parliament is installed. The parliament, to be functional, must be endowed with sufficient legislative power to be listened to and followed by the executive.

The executive needs to fight to execute the program of the people. Each member of the society must be informed of the difficulties, and the challenge to overcome. The separation of the powers between the legislative, the executive and the judiciary is real and effective. All must work together in harmony with the new democratic laws. All of the societal problems and challenges are tackled and solved through the proper democratic channels and due process instead of by force or imposition.

The liberty of the press is properly and fully restored, and the news information starts to flow correctly from the top to the people and verse visa. The management of the national economic and financial system becomes clear and healthy. It can experience poor level of professionalism and technical inefficiencies, but there is no case of fraud or robbery of public funds and the corruption is under control.

Finally, a healthy competition between the political parties, public and private sectors of the society is introduced. The justice system protects and defends the citizenry by ensuring the rule of law. The citizen works honestly to make the society better and stronger. The level of the civic, judicial, and political conscience increases.

The unemployment rate and the insecurity become lower and hope rises in each citizen. Citizenry access to good education, primary health care, water, and electricity increases considerably.

But the system might struggle especially due to lack of sufficient material, technical, and financial means. If care is not taken, this might lead to instability and its dependence on foreign powers. Therefore it is often necessary to organize transparent, free and democratic elections with a precise number of mandates in order to make this new democracy more dynamic.

Being exhausted by the events, certain leaders will try to hang themselves to the system and try to transform the power into private property. Sometimes these leaders will try to modify the laws, by telling others that they are the only capable hands, even though, in reality they are exhausted. Being politically finished, they will play on family, regional, ethnic or religious affinities. They will attempt this game to stop the political competition. If necessary they will cheat to win the election or cancel them entirely if the result does not favor their interests.

Therefore the people must be vigilant to avoid being fooled by its leaders.

This situation occurs often in the newly democratic countries where the leaders accede to the power through free elections by promising even the impossible. For this reason, the people must fight for a true democracy. This is the case in most of the developing countries where democracy is not fully rooted yet. This is why such a society can easily fall back again into dictatorship, depravity or civil war situation.

If the society continues to be managed and governed properly based on democratic principles, then national patriotism will rise again in each citizen. With sustainable political stability and a healthy economy, this society will experience economic expansion that will be followed by a positive outlook and mindset by the population. If the new trend is sustained with a series of well-meaning and minded administration, then a sustainable and productive democratic society becomes a reality.

This is how this society will pass positively to the phase of positive activity.

2. Society of Positive Activity

In this society, on one hand the production is oriented towards the satisfaction of the people intentions and on the other there is a lack of technical and intellectual capabilities to improve and accelerate the production.

This society is characterized by a quick development of the agriculture, communication ways, small and middle enterprises. There is free enterprise in all sectors of the economy. To this development phase, we see the emergence of an active group of small local producers. This is the phase of the popular enrichment and the apparition of a small local bourgeoisie. The wealth is almost equitably shared following the degree of activity of each participant. This society works on the principle of each according to his yield. The worker is at the decision, execution and division of the produced wealth. The power assures the protection of its citizens while offering the same chances to all citizens. The political power has to guarantee a low cost of energetic resources and raw materials in order to increase the economic activity.

The political power must encourage citizens in entrepreneurship by granting them some financial funds. It should have a policy of absorption of the surplus of production in order to maintain and empower small businessmen in villages and remote areas. It also must guarantee the security of citizen wealth and favor the exchanges with the exterior. It must reinforce the justice and the democratic institutions in order to avoid the corruption and the dictatorship. As well as the unemployment rate will diminish; we will attend to the arrival of a first wave of foreign immigrants. If this society succeeds, it becomes an exporter of goods to the conquest of knowledge. This society forms itself only from the well managed societies of positive will, where the citizens become at the same time workers, auctioneers, deciders and owners of certain enterprises. Therefore, the leaders should be effectively intellectual patriots. With time, this society will be obliged to import qualified foreign intellectuals to form technically and intellectually its citizens in order to develop the country. It is only by this way that this society can pass to the phase of positive knowledge.

3. Society of The Positive Knowledge

This is a society where the activity is oriented towards the acquisition of knowledge, techniques and technologies. This society succeeds to the one of the positive activity. The leaders of this society are obliged to spend a very big part of national income to import foreign intellectual people to build schools, universities and research centers.

This society is characterized by the importation of qualified labor in order to form intellectually the local population. These foreigners will come and reside there with their families. Some of them will decide to reside permanently. Others will form families with the autochthons. So we assist to the arrival of a new wave of educated and qualified workers. This new wave of immigrants will radically influence the life of this society. They will succeed in changing the mentalities of this population.

We will see the apparition of a new culture, mentalities, religious sects and behaviors. This new culture in some cases will enter in contradiction with the local culture. This new culture will be more dynamic, better adapted to the reality. This new culture will be the principal force of the development of this society.

With time, the descendants of these immigrants will be entire citizens of this society.

They will play a very important role in political, social and economic life of this society. They will participate in the demolition of the old culture. They will play an important role for the passage of this society from the phase of positive knowledge to the one of the positive power.

Let's recognize that sometime this cultural change does not occur easily because it requires a complete denial of the previous one.

4. Society of Positive Power

Society where the intention of the leaders is not in harmony with the one of the people, while there are enough material, financial, intellectual and technical means to realize this intention. The leaders may sometimes hide their real objectives.

In this society the leaders may come to the power democratically or by using force. These leaders take the power in order to make financial and material gains or in order to revenge or to express some affirmation.

Here we have different groups of monopolists ruling from the top. This is a corrupted political class that works for itself or for a group that is located outside the country. It's a society of insecurity, injustice and social inequality where each member thinks for himself.

The importance of each member of the society is expressed through his material and financial resources. For this reason, we call this society, the society of power confrontation because it works to serve the rich people.

In the long run this society may encounter a big economic crisis. This crisis will be created by the rivalries that exist between these leading groups and the ones that exist between the rich and the poor.

These rivalries can lead to a struggle between different groups or to a war between different nations for a gain of new markets or raw materials.

To progress, this society should pass to the phase of positive resource. So they will need the arrival of patriots to power. Once in power these patriots should fight against corruption and insecurity. They should reinstate the democratic process in the political life. They should fight against the existing monopoles. They should stimulate the economic growth and involve the government in the process of the regulation of the private business.

Finally the leaders should reduce the gap existing between the rich and the poor and stimulate the production on a large scale. After that this society will pass to the phase of positive resource.

5. Society of Positive Resource

This society exists in the industrialized countries where every person is obliged to sell his will and his knowledge to get financial gains. This society is formed from a transformation of the society of positive power. It is characterized by a recovery of the production and the consumption on a large scale. This is due largely to the elaboration of new laws that regularize the concurrence.

It's the implication of the government in the regulation of markets that later leads to a surplus of production in the sectors of nutrition and lodging. If well managed, this society will become a society of large scale production and consumption.

At this phase of development, the policy of the leaders will be the research of markets to evacuate the production surplus. At this time, the demographic potential will play a positive role since it will help to absorb the local production. The consumer citizens begin to have access to the luxury product. This is the time of apparition of a middle class well connected, formed of semi-rich and intellectual people. This group will play a very important role in the political life of this society.

This group will participate actively to the elections at any level. If this society continues to progress, it will pass to the phase of positive conscience.

6. Society of Positive Conscience

In this society the leaders have an intention that is in harmony with the one of the people. They also have the technical and intellectual knowledge for the realization of the intention of the people. But these leaders collide themselves with some material and financial difficulties.

This is a society of popular conscience or national conscience.

This society may be formed after the phase of large scale production and consumption when the people will be better informed to know exactly what they want and how to reach their goals. Here the laws are clearer since better elaborated.

This society may also be formed from an ancient happy society that suffers of material damage followed by an economic recession but succeeded to maintain its technical performances and democratic institutions. These calamities can be caused by natural disaster such as earthquakes, volcanoes, floods or war.

The strength of this society resides on its technological performances and democratic institutions. All democratic and state structures are stable at this phase. Each member knows his rights and duties. Here the conscious members of the society have access to wealth and the rich are held to be conscious and honest. The people effectively work for their happiness and their freedom. The democratic system becomes a reality.

Here painters, artists find their real place. In the long run this society becomes freer and happier.

Education, healthcare, lodging, job, food and means of displacement for everybody become a reality. The national wealth of this society is not due to the exploitation of mineral resources but to the technical, technological and scientific performances in management, communication, marketing and production.

In the long run this society will pass to the phase of freedom and real happiness if it succeeds to expand correctly its economic growth.

7. Society of Happiness And Freedom

In this society, the leaders come to power through free and democratic elections to execute the intention freely expressed of a conscious people. This is a democratic society in economical progression and in harmonious development of all sectors. In this society there is a separation of all the powers. To accede to the power the candidates make free electoral campaign and the people choose them following their programs. Each member of the society can lead a harmonious life with others and the nature. The level of the moral, juridical and political conscience is very high. Any member can have good vacations and wealth by working honestly.

The economic production is in perpetual growth and the society is in perpetual progression. The investments in the scientific research are very high. The incomes of the engineers, seekers are very high. There is a harmonious liaison between the priority of the development and the scientific research orientation. There are good relations between the employers and the employees.

Life is oriented towards the emancipation of each member of this society. Any competition is made with the respect of law. This is a society of law where all human rights are respected. Almost everyone works by love and the wealth is equitably shared following the principle. Each member should get what he deserves. The justice system works correctly and public funds are well managed. There is almost no corruption and misappropriation of public funds. Like any other societies, this society can make some positive transformations or be in trouble.

- If well managed, this society will pass to a new structure qualitatively superior (Trans-society}
- It might be that corrupt people come democratically to the power. So these corrupt people set the corruption and the society falls in the negative.
- It might also be that the leaders put the society in war against others for hegemony of interests. If this society loses the war, it can find itself with a big material, financial and intellectual destruction. So this society enters again in the negative.
- This society may also fall in a society of positive conscience if it goes through some natural calamities such earthquakes, volcanoes, but succeeds to maintain its technical performances and democratic institutions.

DESCRIPTION OF THE SOCIETIES OF THE NEGATIVE

8. Society of Neutrality of The People

This society is characterized by the existence of a completely submissive population and a group of persons called party, clan, family, colonizers that exploit the people. Between these 2 groups, there is a third group of technicians that forms a very powerful repressive machine that works for the dictators.

The societal production is oriented towards the satisfaction of needs of the repressive powers and dictators. No one can escape the control of the machine. The leaders do not answer to the people. The population executes the intention of the leaders. There is no freedom of the press. Public information is geared towards the interests of the leaders. Education system is structured to suite the ideology and interests of the leading class. Power is structured to go around within the privilege class. Economic and financial system are not properly structured and as such, they do not exist. As a result, government accountability becomes a thing of fiction, and state fund is therefore mostly channeled towards satisfying the ruling class. Justice system becomes unaccountable, controlled, and big political prisons are built for the purpose of incarcerating or quieting political oppositions, and the process is perpetual.

The leaders are above the law. Everything is done in the name of the people. Only the leaders have access to money and therefore only they can make some misappropriation acts.

In this society there are 3 groups of interests; the interests of the real leaders: dictators or exploiters, the interests of the repressive machine: police, militia, army, state security, and the interests of the common people.

This type of society exists all over the world. This is a closed society that works for the leaders that reside within or outside of the society. Its disintegration is always as a result of dissension between the members of the class in power since the people is neutral. A dissension among the high level leaders polarizes them and obliges the repressive machine to make its choice by cooperating with some of them against the others. The leaders may be in the same location or abroad. They may be of the same race with the submissive people or not. But the people always live with the repressive machine. The repressive machine may be composed of foreigners or locals. For these reasons we will classify these Dictatorship societies in four types.

Dictator's Origin	Foreign	Foreign	Foreign	Autochthon
Dictator's Residence	Exterior	Interior	Exterior	Interior
Repressive Machine Origin	Foreign	Foreign	Autoch-Thon	Autochthon
Denomination of Submitted People	Populate	Populate	Populate	Populate
Denomination of the Systems	Pure Colonization	Peopling Colonization	Neo Colonization	Local Dictatorship

First type: The leaders of the dictatorship are foreigners residing elsewhere. They come to install by force a repressive machine held by them. They exploit the population with a very rudimentary technology.

This is the pure colonization system.

Second type: The leaders of the dictatorship are foreign conquerors. They install the repressive machine, occupy the lands and reside there indefinitely. They build roads, housings and factories. They use an advanced technology. They establish a segregation based on the differences of race, color, or religion.

We call it a peopling colonization.

Third type: The leaders of the dictatorship are people that reside abroad. They install a repressive machine composed of the autochthon people. They install a monarchy or a presidential system tailored to their measures.

This is the neo colonization.

Fourth type: The leaders of the dictatorship are autochthons that work for themselves. They establish a repressive machine and a segregation more or less hidden based on political, ethnic, religious, regional or familial affiliations.

This is a local dictatorship.

In this society there is not unemployment since everyone is obliged to work for the dictator. This society is marked by a strong mobilization structure.

9. Society Of Depravaty Or False Happiness

This is a society where the happiness is reduced to a short-term pleasure.

a. This society may be formed from one of the phases of the positive when corruptible persons succeeded in taking power through democratic means or by force.
b. This society may also be formed at the end of the dictatorship when corruptible persons took over the power. In this second case, the new leadership starts liberating the people from any form of control, and forced labor. At the same time, the people stop receiving helps and subsidies from the new authority. The people feel freer and begin to discover the delights of the world. They start traveling abroad, to have access to new opportunities, current information and pleasures. They begin contemplating new horizons and become connected to new technologies and high consumptions. This is the formation of the society of big exchange, consummation and commerce. The population stops taking care of the agriculture and industry. Some of the former members of the repressive machine in the previous administration may find their way back into the government and start collaborate with the new regime, while the rest of their colleagues re-enter the society and join the private sector or become entrepreneurs.

Those of them who succeeded in finding their way back into the government will change their method of action, and strategy; they become better equipped, and informed, relatively less controlling and numerically smaller. Each of them works to position himself well in order to maximize every opportunity that comes his way.

In time, the lack of discipline enters in the new administration. This is the new period of misappropriation of public funds. And here comes the corruption, unemployment, illicit enrichment by the leaders and the exhibition of their wealth. This situation is followed by a decrease in societal production output, economic meltdown, and currency devaluation.

As the wealth decreases, people will start struggling to maintain their standard of living. To achieve that, some people will strive to create fake situations by designing, creating and perpetuating fraud and corruption. And this marks the appearance of bad conscience among the population.

As things continue to tighten up, some people aware of the irresponsibility of the government, and the resulting crushing hardship hitting the populace, becomes the brain of a new Mafia.

They, together with some of the known bad people form a new band of criminal. Some of them use their old relationships with those in power to make money by misappropriating the public funds without any control. This is the apparition of new Richs.

In this society, becoming wealthy in an honest way becomes impossible, because the system in place will never allow you to genuinely achieve success. The honest worker has no chance to success. The only justice that works is the one of the corrupt. The honest intellectuals live a life of desolation and depravity in order to forget their concerns.

With a big number of unemployment, the population lives a life of deprivation. This society is characterized by the existence of general deprivation at all levels. Drug, alcohol, corruption, injustice, robbery, unemployment, and insecurity become the order of the day.

This is a system which is very easy to build and perpetuate. With a lack of economic production output, and mounting unrest among the population, the leadership attempt to return the population to dictatorship. They will institute constraining and anti-democratic structures such as pressure on opposition, state control of news information, and the intimidation and suppression of the population.

It is possible to quit this system through genuine democratization of the society or through a revolution. If the population and the patriotic forces remain inactive, the leaders will reestablish the dictatorship. These leaders know that they will lose the power if they organize free, democratic, and transparent elections.

Being aware of the consequences of their irresponsible leadership makes them never to want to go. The administration tries to remain in power at any cost while looking out for their interests. They reinforce their individual securities and transfer their stolen funds to safe havens abroad. The society becomes a fully-fledged dictatorship if the leaders systematically succeed in eliminating the opposition.

This society can transform itself into a society of positive will if free and democratic elections are organized (which is impossible). This is why over time; this society will pass to the phase of revolt, shock, and revolution.

10. Society of Revolt And Revolution

In this society, we have a small group of people who takes advantage of the available resources, and a big, poor and miserable majority of the population that have lost hope for a better future. There are only 2 acting groups:

A leadership with a powerless and unpopular repressive machine, and a population dedicated to end the situation of submission and depravity.

The cause of the advent of a revolution resides in the decrease of the standard of living of the citizens, and the hopelessness of a better future. One of the causes of the acceleration of the advent of a revolution is the increasingly blatant contradiction between the available resources for the happiness of the society and their use to perpetuate the servitude of the people. Because of the nature of the politics and the urgency of the crises, the people is left with no better choice than to radically break with the existing structures and remove the leadership by force.

This is marked by popular revolt, followed by general disobedience. This is the time of strikes, sabotage, non-submission, sometimes robberies, arson, deaths, and arrests until the removal of the leadership.

As a result, the real power leaves the leadership and resides with the people. At the beginning, the existing leaderships will attempt to reprimand the population, but after excessive fights, it will lose and will disappear from the power wheels. This is the end of the revolt and the advent of revolution. And the people will start to find hope again for a brighter better future. (Note that if the popular disobedience does not succeed, this movement becomes just a revolt and the leadership reprimands the rebels).

The revolution allows the demolition of the existing power with all its structures.

It can take place at the end of a dictatorship era. In this case, the support of the international community is necessary to form and support the conquerors.

It can occur at the end of a depravity era and allows the passage to the phase of positive will, if democratic patriots drive it. Once in power, these patriots should establish a democratic system and the revolution would be called a democratic revolution.

New dictators or other corrupt people can also usurp this revolution. For this reason, the population must be very vigilant to always control those that have the power.

Revolution is necessary in non-democratic or pseudo democratic societies. This is why the revolutions occur frequently in societies of depravity.

3.2 Dynamic Of The Group Of The Negative

Now we will pass to a detailed study of the sphere of the negative to comprehend all its possible transitions. It is necessary to notice that more than half of the World's countries are in the negative. This study will show us the way to follow to get out of the negative, and the history of certain countries that passed many decades in this position without so far getting out.

Let's start by presenting the structure of the block of the negative and its dynamic in general.

Here are the three phases of the negative (dictatorships, false happiness and revolt) and the first phase of the positive (positive will). It's what we call the bloc of the Negative. Each transition corresponds to a number.

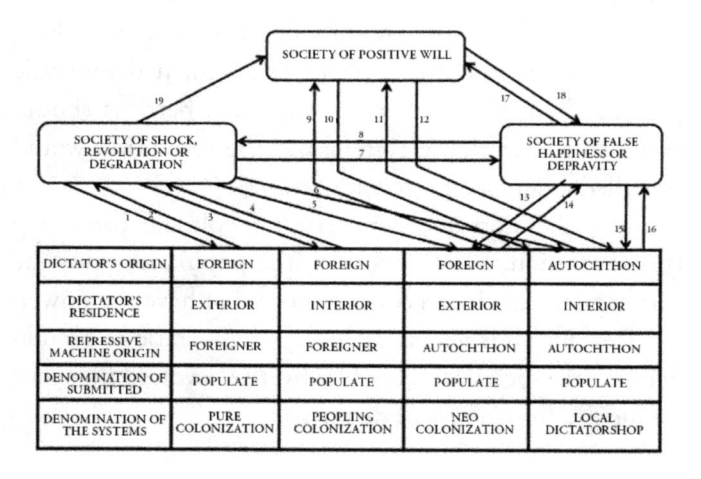

DICTATOR'S ORIGIN	FOREIGN	FOREIGN	FOREIGN	AUTOCHTHON
DICTATOR'S RESIDENCE	EXTERIOR	INTERIOR	EXTERIOR	INTERIOR
REPRESSIVE MACHINE ORIGIN	FOREIGNER	FOREIGNER	AUTOCHTHON	AUTOCHTHON
DENOMINATION OF SUBMITTED	POPULATE	POPULATE	POPULATE	POPULATE
DENOMINATION OF THE SYSTEMS	PURE COLONIZATION	PEOPLING COLONIZATION	NEO COLONIZATION	LOCAL DICTATORSHOP

1. War for pure colonization establishment.

This test is observed when armies troops, made essentially of foreign invaders use weapons to kick out the autochthons from power. They install a repressive machine made essentially of foreigners. They exploit the local people. This transition occurs with bloodshed considering the non-popularity of the invaders.

2. War for the suppression of pure colonization.

This is an armed war that takes place inside a society of pure colonization. This war will end with the taking of power by a group made of the first inhabitants of this country. If the new leaders drive the country to the phase of positive will, we will say that they made a democratic revolution. If they establish depravity, or neo-colonization, or dictatorship regime, we will say that they lead a war for the establishment of depravity or neo-colonization, or dictatorship.

3. War for establishment of peopling colonization.

This test is observed when armies troops, made essentially of foreign invaders use weapons to kick out the autochthons from power. They install a repressive machine composed only of invaders. They occupy the lands of the locality. They reside there. These invaders import their modern techniques and exploit the local people. This transition takes place always with a bloodshed considering the non-popularity of the invaders.

4. War for peopling colonization suppression.

This is an armed war that occurs inside a peopling colonization society. This war will end with the retaking power by the autochthons. If the new leaders drive the country to the positive will regime, we will say that they made a democratic revolution. If these new leaders establish depravity or neo-colonization, or local dictatorship regime, we will say that they made a war for depravity or neo-colonization, or local dictatorship establishment.

5. War for the establishment of neo-colonization.

This test occurs when an armed group in common agreement with foreign country takes the power by war. These new leaders establish a repressive machine composed of autochthons and make the people work for the country that supported them.

6. War for local dictatorship imposition.

This event happens when an armed group of autochthons by the force of weapons takes the power in a country, which is already in war. These new leaders install a dictatorships regime and they make the people work for them.

7. War for establishment of the depravity.

This test is observed when an armed group by war takes the power and succeeds to impose the depravity.

8. Passage from the depravity phase to the revolt.

This event occurs when the people organize a popular uprising against a corrupted system. We call this event revolt if this people do not succeed to kick out the corrupted leaders from power. We call this event, misappropriated revolution if this uprising succeeds to kick out the former leaders from power without establishing a democratic regime. We call this event-democratic revolution if the uprising changes completely the former leaders and succeeds to build a democratic regime.

9. Passage from neo-colonization to positive will.

This positive test takes place when the neo-colonizers, under pressure of national and international communities or simply by loss of economic and strategic interests, decide to organize free and democratic elections. They organize elections knowing that they will lose them in advance. This positive test occurs also when armed group, without bloodshed succeeds to take the power and to organize free and democratic elections. They destroy the repressive machine and allow the arrival of democrat patriots to power.

10. Passage from the positive will to neo-colonization.

This event arrives when an armed group in common agreement with a foreign country, without bloodshed, takes a power held by patriots leaders elected democratically. This event occurs also when a group of people working for foreign interests democratically takes the power. These new leaders liquidate the political parties, they establish a repressive machine and they make the people work to satisfy the interests of this foreign country.

11. Passage from the local dictatorship to the positive will.

This positive passage takes place when dictators, under pressure of national and international communities decide to organize free and democratic elections. They organize elections generally lost in advance and accept the verdict of the urns. The dictator gives the power to the new elected leaders. This positive test occurs also when armed group takes the power and organizes free and democratic elections without bloodshed. This society passes to the phase of positive will if these new leaders are patriot democrats.

12. Passage from the positive will to the local dictatorship.

This passage happens when an armed group without bloodshed takes a power held by patriots leaders elected democratically. This transition occurs also when dictators democratically take the power. These new leaders liquidate the political parties, they establish a dictatorship regime and they make the people work for them.

13. Passage from the depravity to neo-colonization.

This transition takes place when a foreign power, for strategic or economic reasons succeeds to protect leaders of corrupted system in order to establish the neo-colonization. These new leaders eliminate the political parties, they establish a repressive machine and they make the people work to satisfy the interests of the neo-colonizers.

14. Passage from the neo-colonization to depravity.

This event arrives when the neo-colonizer for new priorities decides to abandon a country while giving the power to a local corruptible group. This passage occurs also when a group of armed and corruptible people succeeds to take the power from the neo-colonizer without bloodshed. These new leaders establish the depravity as model of development.

15. Passage from the depravity to the local dictatorship

This event takes place when a group of corrupted leaders in loss of force and credibility succeeds to impose its dictate. This transition occurs also when a group of armed dictators succeeds to kick out a corrupted regime from power without bloodshed. This group succeeds to close the press, the media, opposition parties and to impose a dictatorship regime.

16. Passage from the local dictatorship to the depravity.

This test is observed when an autochthon dictator under pressure gives democratically the power to corruptible persons. This test occurs also when a group of armed and corruptible people succeeds to take the power from the dictators without bloodshed. These new leaders establish the depravity as model of development.

17. Passage from the depravity to positive will.

This test takes place when a corrupted system under interior and exterior pressure decides to organize transparent, free and democratic elections. It is important to note that these corrupted leaders will attempt to manipulate the results of the elections in their favor especially if they have their own candidate. Therefore the people should take its responsibilities. This event occurs also when an armed group of patriotic and democratic forces succeeds to take the power without bloodshed. Once in power, they build a democratic regime. This change is possible only when non-corrupt patriot, non-involved in the former system get the political power.

18. Passage from the positive will to depravity.

This transition arrives when an armed corruptible group without bloodshed takes a power held by patriots leaders elected democratically. This test occurs also when corruptible group democratically takes the power. These new leaders establish the depravity as model of development.

19. Revolutionary passage to the positive will.

This event occurs when a people living in the negative organize a popular uprising and succeed to kick out his leaders from power. The people establish a democratic regime and patriots arrive to the power. This is what we call democratic revolution.

3.3 CONCLUSION

In conclusion we can say that in society's life, we have the following points.

1. There are 7 successive and progressive phases. These positive phases are the intention I, the activity A, the knowledge K, the power P, the resources R, the conscience C, the accomplishment or freedom F. Between the successive positive phases it exists always the three phases of the negative that thread the positive evolution. The

3 phases of the negative bloc are the submission, the depravity, and the chock and revolt.
2. Each of these phases is qualitatively superior to the previous one.
3. The succession of phases cannot be avoided in the accomplishment of a positive evolution. This is why a society cannot go from the positive knowledge to the positive conscience without going through the positive power and the positive possession respectively.
4. Each phase can only be prepared and determined from the phase that precedes it directly. Therefore, the degree of happiness and freedom of a society depends on its conscience. The phase of the positive conscience of a society depends on its resources. The phase of the positive resources of a society depends on its power. The phase of a positive power of a society depends on its knowledge. The phase of a positive knowledge of a society depends on its activity. The phase of the positive activity of a society depends on its intention and will.
5. If it does not follow this established order the society falls into the negative because it will lack the required material and spiritual bases.
6. When in disharmony with the conditions of its environment, a society can easily remain in the negative until its degradation or total demolition if it refuses categorically to return to the phase corresponding to its level. However if it realizes soon that it is in the negative, it will return

to the phase that corresponds to its real level. This return can be done by revolution or by negotiated passage.
7. A society cannot regress without the action of an external constraining force. In this condition of submission, the society will always fight to reach the phase that corresponds to its level. This passage also can be done by revolution that drives to the brutal disappearance of this constraining force or by negotiated passage.
8. Thus after many tests of evolution and revolution it can arrive to the 7th phase called accomplishment.

Once in this phase it will feel really happy and free. As life is a succession of actions, this society will start again a new action and so on until it reaches the seventh positive phase of the seventh action.

To this phase, it will pass to a new structure qualitatively superior, Post-Society.

CHAPTER 4

Evolution of Humanity

In this part, we will prove the existence and the smooth working of the triad's law in the life of humanity under its dynamic form. Therefore, we will use the stairs of evolution of humanity to detect the presence of the 7 phases of its positive evolution.

Let's start with the detection of these 7 phases in their order of succession.

1. Phase of Positive Will and Negative Power– Primitive community Society.
2. Phase of Positive Activity and Negative Knowledge– Exploitation Society.
3. Phase of Positive Knowledge and Negative Activity– Feudal Society.
4. Phase of Positive Power and Negative Will– Pure-Capitalist Society.
5. Phase of Positive Resource and Negative Conscience– Society of High Production and Large Consumption.
6. Phase of Positive Conscience and Negative Resource– Society of Major Social Reforms.
7. Phase of happiness and Freedom– Society of accomplishment.

4.1 Description Of The 7 Phases Of The Evolution Of Humanity

First phase of evolution of our humanity that corresponds to the positive will or Intention. (Primitive community)

In this phase, people pooled their good will because they were helpless in front of the nature and the surrounding world. They were forced to work together, gather, hunt and protect themselves. Those who succeeded to show more courage and commitment became the leaders of this society. This "awakening" of the braves led to the second phase of development which is the positive activity.

Second phase of evolution of humanity that corresponds to the positive activity. (Society of exploitation)

In this phase, people led their activities because they were without knowledge. This is the time of the discovery of agriculture, private property, demarcation of territory, trade, etc. The luckiest people succeeded to made production tools and became the leaders. These owners of the means of production used the physical forces of the other members to satisfy their personal interests. Thus there appeared two classes.

- The class of owners of means of production or leading class.
- The class of non-owners of means of production or exploited class. It's the revolution of the most active (luckiest) people that led to the third phase of development which is the positive knowledge.

Third phase of evolution of humanity which corresponds to the positive Knowledge (Feudal society from 481-1750)

In this phase, people put their knowledge and experiences in competition. This is the phase of the apparition and expansion of science, technology, culture and religion. The holders of knowledge (culture, science, technology and religion) became the leaders of this society. They took advantage of the lack of education of other members to satisfy their personal interests.

In this society we have two classes:

- The class of holders of positive knowledge or leading class (clergy and nobility).
- The class of non-holders of positive knowledge or oppressed class (peasants).

This was the time of the technical development, trade and race for money. It is this technological revolution that led to the fourth phase of development which is the positive power.

Fourth phase of evolution of humanity that corresponds to the positive power. (Society of pure and hard capitalism 1860-1960)

In this phase, people put their power (technical and religious knowledge, material and financial wealth) in competition. The winners become the leaders and they use others to satisfy their personal interests. In this society we have two classes:

- The class of the powerful people or the leading class.
- The class of the powerless people or exploited class.

People use their creativity and invention to increase the productivity. The revolution of this power is leading our humanity to the fifth phase of development which is the positive resource.

Fifth phase of evolution of humanity corresponds to the positive resource. (Society of large production and consumption- 1960 to present)

At this stage, people put in competition their ability to obtain a positive resource. Those who manage to produce and sell in big scale become the leaders. They use other people to satisfy their own interests.

In this society emerge two classes:

- The class of holders of resource or leading class.
- The class of non-holders of resource or exploited class.

Presently much of the population (middle class) of the countries of the West of Europe and North of America reach this standard of living. If in the previous phase we should work to meet our needs, in this new one we work to spend (consume) and run the system. If Descartes used to say "I think therefore I am", now it is "I spend, therefore I am".

The export of new production methods (advanced technology), and the sale of goods and services of the Western countries created the globalization. Currently, globalization is eliminating distances, weakening the boundaries for all types of migration. Working conditions of an individual are increasingly determined by what happens on the entire planet.

The revolution of the globalization is leading some Western European, North American and some Asian countries to the sixth phase of the positive development which is the positive conscience.

Sixth phase of evolution of humanity that corresponds to the positive conscience. (Society of major social reforms)

At this stage, people put in competition their Consciences (Creativity and ability to communicate and analyze in order to decide). The winners become the leaders and they manage the assets of others.

In this society we also have two classes.

- The class of holders of positive Conscience or leading class.
- The class of non-holders of positive Conscience or the oppressed.

It is a society of great social reforms. Then, countries that possess a positive conscience will universalize (super globalize) this lifestyle and move to the seventh phase of positive development which is the happiness and freedom.

Seventh phase of evolution of humanity that corresponds to the happiness and freedom. (Society of accomplishment)

At this stage, people put in competition their degree of accomplishment and freedom (Capacity to achieve goals positively). The most accomplished become the leaders. In this society we have two classes:

- The class of accomplished or leading class.
- The class of those who are in process of accomplishment.

It is the society of freedom and happiness.

After this phase, humanity will rise to a qualitatively new structure (Trans-humanity).

4.2 Conclusion

In conclusion we can say that in human life, we have the following points.

There are 7 successive and progressive phases.

These positive phases are the intention I, the activity A, the knowledge K, the power P, the resource R, the conscience C, the accomplishment L. Between the successive positive phases, it always exists the three phases of the negative. These phases are the neutrality, the depravity and the shock.

Each of these phases is qualitatively superior to the previous phase.

The succession of these phases cannot be avoided in the accomplishment of a positive evolution. This is why the humanity cannot go from the positive knowledge to the positive conscience without passing through the positive power and the positive resource respectively.

Each phase can only be prepared and determined from the one that precedes it directly. Therefore, the degree of happiness and freedom of humanity depends on its conscience. The phase of the positive conscience of a humanity depends on its resource. The phase of the positive resource of humanity depends on its power. The phase of a positive power of humanity depends on its knowledge. The phase of a positive knowledge of humanity depends on its activity. The phase of the positive activity of humanity depends on its intention and will.

If it does not follow this established order, humanity falls into the negative because it will lack the required material and spiritual bases. When in disharmony with the conditions of its environment, the humanity can easily remain in the negative until its degradation or total demolition, if it refuses categorically to return to the phase corresponding to its level.

However, if it perpetuates in the negative, it will be totally demolished. If it realizes soon that it is in the negative, it can return to the phase that corresponds to its level. This return can be done by revolution or by negotiated passage.

The humanity cannot regress without the support of an external constraining force. In this condition of submission, the humanity will always fight to reach the phase that corresponds to its level. This passage can also be done by revolution that drives to the brutal disappearance of this constraining force or by negotiated passage.

So, after several tests of evolution and revolution, the humanity can arrive to the 7th phase called accomplishment. Once in this phase the humanity will be happy and free. As life is a succession of actions, the humanity will start again a new action and so on until it reaches the seventh positive phase of the seventh action.

To this phase, the humanity will pass to a new structure qualitatively superior.

CHAPTER 5

Signs of Zodiac:

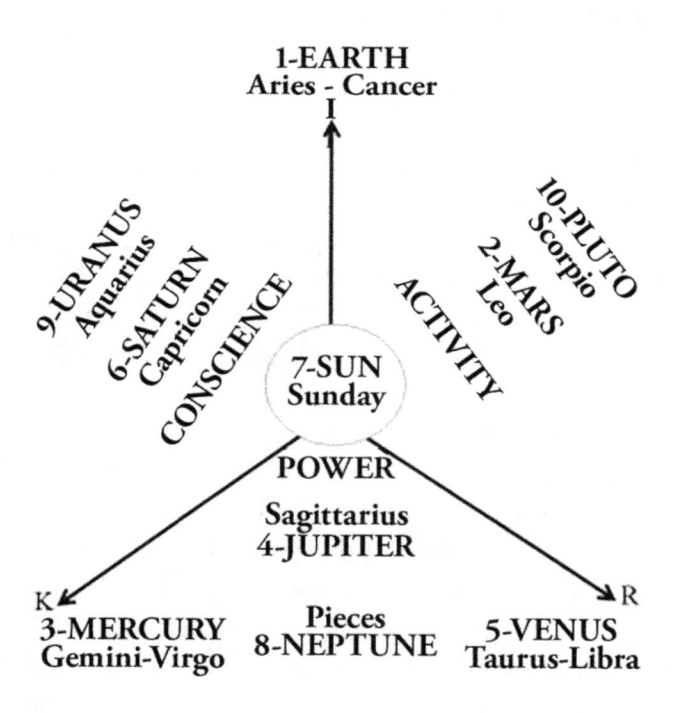

1-EARTH
Aries - Cancer

9-URANUS Aquarius
6-SATURN Capricorn
CONSCIENCE

10-PLUTO Scorpio
2-MARS Leo
ACTIVITY

7-SUN
Sunday

POWER

Sagittarius
4-JUPITER

3-MERCURY
Gemini-Virgo

Pieces
8-NEPTUNE

5-VENUS
Taurus-Libra

In this part, we will apply the triad law to the zodiac. We will explain logically how to find the different zodiac signs. We know that the astrologers consider that each planet has its state of soul and a period of influence during each year. They also consider that each planet plays a role on the future characters of a person being born during its period of influence.

Depending on the orientations of the six positive planets toward the visible and invisible worlds, they have found 12 possibilities. So they divided the year in 12 equal parts. And they consider that each of these 12 parts corresponds to one sign of the zodiac.

It should be noted that the positive planets are Earth, Mars, Mercury, Jupiter, Venus, and Saturn while the negative are Neptune, Uranus and Pluto.

In each sign we let emerge three types of relations. The first type of relation is based on the link existing between the planet and its state of soul. The second type of relation defines in which world the given planet is oriented.

The third type of relation defines the behavior of person when he adopts one of these orientations.

To each orientation of a planet or group of planets correspond one sign of the zodiac. It arrives sometime, that one of the three planets of the negative becomes very influent. For this reason, we can find sometime two dominating planets for only one sign.

5.1 Period Of Influence Of Signs

	PERIOD OF INFLUENCE					*ZODIAC SIGNS*
1	MAR	21	to	APR	19	**Aries**
2	APR	20	to	MAY	20	**Taurus**
3	MAY	21	to	JUN	21	**Gemini**
4	JUN	22	to	JUL	22	**Cancer**
5	JUL	23	to	AUG	22	**Leo**

6	AUG	23	to	SEP	22	Virgo
7	SEP	23	to	OCT	23	Libra
8	OCT	24	to	Nov	21	Scorpion
9	Nov	22	to	Dec	21	Sagittarius
10	DEC	22	to	JAN	19	Capricorn
11	JAN	20	to	FEB	18	Aquarius
12	FEB	19	to	MAR	20	Pisces

5.2 Description Of The Twelve Signs

Looking to the picture of zodiac signs we can say the following: The planet Earth and its satellite Moon influence Aries and Cancer. Earth is the planet of positive will and negative power. Each of these two signs tends to be courageous in one world of power- the aggressive world and the one of resistance. Aries is courageous in the aggressive world while Cancer is courageous in the world of resistance. For these reasons, we have the following characteristics for each sign.

ARIES (EARTH& MOON, MARS, 21 TO APR 19)

Aries is initiative, capable of new beginning. He has great will power and confidence in himself. He is courageous, confident, enterprising, energetic and striving to be the first. He never accepts defeat. He is oriented towards action and competition. He will keep on fighting and striving until he either succeeds or death overtakes him. He is a natural leader. He tends to be dynamic, impulsive, warlike, aggressive, enthusiastic, assertive and forceful. Some of his interests are himself, challenges of any sort, being a leader, starting things for others to pursue. He should avoid trying to seek immediate satisfaction, to be impatient, uncooperative, tactless, agitate and arrogant. His keyword is action and his quality resides on his courage. For these reasons he is considered to be the pioneer of the zodiac.

CANCER (EARTH& MOON, JUN 22 to JUL 22)

Cancer is very tenacious, intuitive, protective, loyal, emotional, sensitive devoted receptive, supportive, family oriented and combative. Cancers are very loving people. Once the love is begun, he never stops loving. However, they can be very cruel when provoked. Cancer tends to be emotional, sensitive and tenacious. Cancer interests are home, family, love and domestic security. He should avoid being delicate, shy, indulgent, timid, passive and provincial. His key word is tenacity and his quality reposes in his caring. Cancer is considered to be the homemaker of the zodiac.

Analyzing these two cases, we observe that the astrologers are talking about two people having positive will power. To succeed, Aries should be less aggressive while Cancer should be more active.

The planet Mars influences Leo sign while the planets Pluto and Mars influence Scorpio sign. Mars is the planet of positive activity and negative knowledge while Pluto is the one of shock, revolution or degradation. Each of these two signs is very active in one powerful world- the world of power with affection and generosity and the one of power with suspicion. Leo uses his power with affection and generosity while Scorpio uses his power with suspicion. For these reasons, we have the following characteristics for each sign.

LEO (MARS from JUL 23 to AUG 22)

Leo is confident, self-assured, generous, courageous, loyal, enthusiastic, strong willed, creative, determined, ambitious, magnanimous and outspoken. Due to his positive activity, Leo is strongly attracted to the opposite sex. Leo tends to be romantic, domineering, and affectionate. Some Leo interests are children, sport, games, fun, achievement, being in the spotlight and in charge. He should avoid being egotistical, self-important, autocratic, patronizing, blunt and overconfident. His key word is active power and his quality resides on his generosity. For these reasons, Leo is considered to be the entertainer of the zodiac.

SCORPIO (PLUTO& MARS, OCT 24 to NOV21)

Scorpio is courageous, strong willed, decided, resourceful and enigmatic. He has no fear of death. Due to Pluto, he is extremely strong. He is considered to be the most potent for good and for evil. His sex drive is usually very strong. He is not halfway with people. He drives himself hard and usually drives others unmercifully. He is a ruthless enemy or competitor. Scorpio tends to be heroic, forceful, secretive, vindictive, cynical, determined, and suspicious. Some Scorpio's interests are money of others, sex, being the unseen power. Because of his strong emotional drive, he needs to keep his integrity high, otherwise, he falls into undesirable behavior such as violence, jealousy, hatred, possessiveness, revenge, self-protection, repression and cruelty. His keyword is energy and his quality is excessive dedication.

Analyzing these two cases, we observe that the astrologers are talking about two people having positive activity. To succeed, Leo should be less overconfident while Scorpio should be less vindictive.

Looking to the picture of zodiac signs we can say the following:

The planet Mercury influences Virgo and Gemini signs. Mercury is the planet of positive knowledge and negative activity. Each of these two signs tends towards one world of knowledge- the world of practical knowledge or the one of theoretic knowledge. Virgo is oriented to the practical knowledge while Gemini is oriented to the theoretic one. For these reasons, we have the following characteristics for each sign.

VIRGO (MERCURY from AUG 23 to SEP 22)

Virgo is constantly to the knowledge research. He is exact, organized, efficient, methodical, thorough, modest, analytical, responsible and attentive. He tends to be critical, methodical, neat, reliable and cautious.

Some Virgo's interests are helping to improve others, work-details and perfection. Virgo should avoid being hypercritical, pitying, highly structured, overly skeptical, anxious, timid, so immersed in details and servile. To succeed, he should learn to think only positive thoughts since he is very practical. His keyword is practice and his virtue resides on his thoroughness. For these reasons Virgo is considered to be the craftsperson of the zodiac.

GEMINI (MERCURY from MAY 21 to JUN 21)

Gemini is curious, logical, rational, scientific and skilled with words, eloquent, quick minded, mobile, diverse, knowledgeable and living with present. Gemini tends to be superficial, intelligent and versatile. He is always interested in intellectual activities such as trips, communications, travel, being a know-it-all, learning, writing, talking and reading. To succeed, he should avoid being undisciplined, inconsistent, double dealing, nervous, unreliable, lacking concentration and dishonest. Gemini is considered as the most intelligent of the zodiac. His keyword is variety and his quality resides on his alertness. For these reasons, Gemini is considered to be the salesperson, communicator and the nonconformist of the zodiac.

Analyzing these two cases, we observe that the astrologers are talking about two people having positive knowledge. To succeed, Virgo should be less critical while Gemini should be more disciplined.

The planet Jupiter influences Sagittarius sign while the planets Neptune and Jupiter influence Pisces sign.

Jupiter is the planet of positive power and negative will while Neptune is the one of submission. Each of these two signs tends to be very powerful in one part of the complex world- the real and the imaginary worlds. Sagittarius is powerful in the real world while Pisces is powerful in the imaginary one. For these reasons, we have the following characteristics for each sign.

SAGITTARIUS (JUPITER, NOV 22 to DEC 21)

Sagittarius is generous, amiable, enthusiastic, goal-directed, outdoors-oriented, truth seeker and discerning unlighted. He always seems to be helped by some protective shield. He tends to be optimistic, friendly, easy-going and argumentative. Some Sagittarius interests are religion, philosophy, traveling, law, books, giving advice. He should avoid being pretentious, impractical, extravagant, hypocritical, blindly optimistic, unrealistic and impatient. He should also learn to respect restrictions. His key word is freedom and his quality resides on his hopefulness. Sagittarius is considered to be the philosopher of the zodiac since he wants to know the objective world and its laws.

PISCES (NEPTUNE- JUPITER, FEB 19 to MAR 20)

He is an imaginary creative, spiritual, visionary, gentle, sympathetic, trusting and easy to please.

Influenced by Neptune, he becomes adaptable, accepting sensitive and submissive in the real world. Pisces always wants to do the right things. He alternates between pessimism and optimism. He seems to be turned on to world of dreams. He has over active imagination. He tends to be sensitive, impressionable, compassionate, changeable, daydreaming and dependent. Some of his interests are just thinking, serving others and drugs. He should avoid being unrealistic, imprudent, submissive, vague, confused and overly responsive. His keyword is compassion and his quality is charity. Pisces is considered to be the martyr of the zodiac.

Analyzing these two cases, we observe that the astrologers are talking about two people having positive power. To succeed, Sagittarius should be more balancing while Pieces should be more realistic.

The planet Venus influences Libra and Taurus signs. Venus is the planet of positive resource and negative conscience. Each of these two signs tends towards one world of resource- the world of balanced resource or the one of unbalanced resource. Balanced resource means resource obtained by taking into consideration the interests of both sides while unbalanced resource means the contrary. Libra is oriented to the balanced world of resource while Taurus is oriented to the unbalanced one. For these reasons, we have the following characteristics for each sign.

LIBRA (VENUS from SEP 23 to OCT 23)

Libra is relationship oriented, sharing and mediating person. He is peace loving, tactful, diplomatic, agreeable and charming. He is a good counselor and judge because he can clearly see both sides of an issue. However this ability to see an issue, from all sides, gives him a problem of making decision especially concerning minor matters. He wants to have a strong sense of justice and fair play. Libra tends to be, romantic, dependent, and cooperative. Libra interests are peace, beauty, partnerships, justice, social life and companionships. He should avoid being indecisive, overly compromising, unreal, fear for own benefit, dishonest, and dependent. His key word is harmony and his quality resides in his fairness. Libra is considered to be the diplomat of the zodiac.

TAURUS (VENUS from APR 20 to MAY 20)

Taurus is loyal, devoted, self-sufficient, stable, reliable, solid, persistent, resolute and patient. He pursues with great zest everything that will satisfy his desire. He likes beautiful things and usually focuses his energy on acquiring material resources and money. He is somehow slow, but always finishes what he starts. His characteristics are materialism, greed, laziness, patience, practicality and endurance. Some of his interests are comfort, money and resource of all sorts. Due to his negative conscience, he can be jealous to the extreme. Taurus should avoid being possessive, unspiritual, immovable and unchanging. His key word is resource and his quality reposes on his reliability. Taurus is considered to be the accumulator and builder of zodiac.

Analyzing these two cases, we observe that the astrologers are talking about two people having positive resources. To succeed, Libra should decide quickly while Taurus should be less jealous.

The planet Saturn influences Capricorn while the planets Uranus and Saturn influence Aquarius.

Saturn is the planet of positive conscience and negative resource, while Uranus is the one of false happiness. Each of these two signs tends to be very conscious toward one world- the personal material and the humanitarian worlds. Capricorn is oriented to the individual material world while Aquarius is oriented to the social humanitarian one. For these reasons, we have the following characteristics for each sign.

CAPRICORN (SATURNE, DEC22 to JAN 19)

He is serious, frugal, hardworking and determined to achieve his goals. He is practical, patient, persistent and cautious. He will let nothing stand on his way. He is an indefectible enemy and loyal friend. Capricorn is considered by the astrologers to be the strongest sign of the zodiac. He tends to be serious, ambitious, realistic, cautious responsible. Some Capricorn interest are business, material success and being in charge. Because of his positive conscience, if he maintains integrity, he can achieve the highest of accomplishment. If he lacks integrity by orienting negatively his intention, he can also achieve his goals, but then he will have a great fall. He should avoid being authoritarian, exploitative, materialistic and condescending. His key word is ambition and he like to be respected. For these reasons, Capricorn is considered to be manager of the zodiac.

AQUARIUS (URANUS, SATURNE JAN 20- FEB 18)

Aquarius is the sign of friendship and brotherhood. He is intellectual, loyal, scientific and truth seeker. He is a tireless worker and prefers to work in some sphere that has humanitarian benefits. Due to his positive conscience, he is willing to work for what he wants and does not demand more than what he deserves. Some interests of Aquarius are friends, helping others and politics. Because of Uranus influence, he tends to be tactless, independent, eccentric and rebellious. He should avoid being eccentric, dishonest, overly compromising, indecisive and unfair. His key word is independence and his quality is friendship. For these reasons, Aquarius is considered to be the reformer of the zodiac.

Analyzing these two cases, we observe that the astrologers are talking about two people having positive conscience. To succeed, Capricorn should maintain integrity while Aquarius should be less eccentric.

CHAPTER 6

The Creation

Let us comment on the first two chapters of Genesis to demonstrate the existence and functionality of this Triad Law on its static and dynamic forms. Let us show that the 7 days of creation are the same 7 phases of all evolution. It is in fact a code that has been bequeathed to us to achieve a positive evolution. Without going into details here is a brief overview of the days of creation. Each comment will be preceded by the word "Comment".

4.1 Interpretation Of The Two First Chapters Of Genesis By The Triad

THE FIRST DAY

LIGHT	= DIVINE SPIRIT
DAY	= PART ILLUMINATED BY THE DIVINE SPIRIT
GOOD	= POSITIVE
NIGHT	= PART NOT ILLUMINATED BY THE DIVINE SPIRIT

In the beginning God created the heaven and the earth. And the earth was without form, and darkness was upon the face of the deep. And the Spirit of God moved upon the face of the waters. And God said, **Let there be light: and there was light**. And God saw the light, that it was good: and God separated the light from the darkness. **And God called the light Day, and the darkness he called Night.**

And the evening and the morning were the first day.

Comment: This is when the Divine spirit penetrated the Earth. This spirit is transported by the energy of the first three-dimensional cosmic wave. We call this energy carrying the Divine Spirit the soul of the Earth. This cosmic soul or energy carries an intention and a will at the same time. This energy is for the Earth what the heart and the air are for a person at his birth. It is the phase of appearance and activation of the Earth. There was an evening and there was one morning means that there was no dark night but rather a drop in clarity. (No a transit through the negative, but rather a smooth and positive pass). So after a long period of positive evolution, this was the first phase of Earth formation.

The first day corresponds to the phase of positive will and negative power.

THE SECOND DAY

And God said, **<u>Let there be a firmament in the midst of the waters, and let it divide the</u> <u>waters from the waters.</u>** And God made the firmament, and divided the waters which were under the firmament from the waters which were above the firmament: and it was so. And God called the firmament Heaven.

And the evening and the morning were the second day.

<u>Comment:</u> By creating a difference of levels between waters, God created a difference of potential energy between them. This difference of potential energy between the waters is the source of their movements. The waters of regions of high potentials stretch towards the ones of the low potentials. We remark that this second day of the week corresponds to the phase of the Earth's increase in volume and energy by a positive will.

After many years of positive evolution, it was the second phase of Earth's formation.

The second day corresponds to the phase of positive activity and negative knowledge.

THE THIRD DAY

And God said, **Let the waters under the heaven be gathered together unto one place, and let the dry land appear: and it was so.** And God called the dry land Earth; and the gathering together of the waters he called Seas: and God saw that it was good.

And God said, **Let the earth bring forth grass, the herb yielding seed, and the fruit tree yielding fruit after his kind, whose seed is in itself, upon the earth:** and it was so.

And the earth brought forth grass, and herb yielding seed after his kind, and the tree yielding fruit, whose seed was in itself, after his kind: and God saw that it was good.

And the evening and the morning were the third day

Comment: God prepared the lands to do some fields of culture of trees and herbs to spread knowledge. So after a long period of positive evolution, it was the third phase of Earth's formation.

The third day corresponds to the phase of positive knowledge and negative activity.

THE FOURTH DAY

And God said, **Let there be lights in the firmament of the heaven to divide the day from the night; and let them be for signs, and for seasons, and for days, and years:**

And let them be for lights in the firmament of the heaven to give light upon the earth: and it was so. And God made two great lights; **the greater light to rule the day, and the lesser light to rule the night:** he made the stars also.

And God set them in the firmament of the heaven to give light upon the earth, and to rule over the day and over the night, and to divide the light from the darkness: and God saw that it was good.

And the evening and the morning were the fourth day.

Comment: This is the phase of the apparition of our Solar system, other Galaxies, stars, and the achievement of the Universe's construction. That is also the phase of the apparition of the second group of three-dimensional energy. The Earth like any being can connect itself positively or negatively to this cosmic wave following its intention. The solar system is composed of our Sun, its 9 planets and their satellites. This phase corresponds to the apparition of the notion of time, space, speed, movement, energy and power.

God trusted the Earth by giving it a part of decision between the positive and the negative. If the Earth acts positively, he will accumulate a positive energy, while if he acts negatively; he will accumulate a negative energy. After many years of positive evolution, it was the fourth phase of Earth's formation. The fourth day corresponds to the phase of power and negative intention.

THE FIFTH DAY

And God said, **Let the waters bring forth abundantly the moving creature that hath life, and fowl that may fly above the earth in the open firmament of heaven.** And God created great whales, and every living creature that moved, which the waters brought forth abundantly, after their kind, and every winged fowl after his kind: and **God saw that it was good.** And **God blessed them,** saying, Be fruitful, and multiply, and fill the waters in the seas, and let fowl multiply in the earth. And the evening and the morning were the fifth day.

Comment: That is the phase of animals' apparition. These animals appear in the lands and the seas. In animals, we have a new form of resource. That is the produced possession, a new form of matter.

In animals, we have enough matter and a negative (few) conscience. That is the phase of the accumulation of the second group of two-dimensional energy connected to the activity. We see that the fifth day corresponds to the apparition of production of wealth and animal reproduction.

This is the phase of the positive possession and negative conscience.

THE SIXTH DAY

And God said, Let the earth bring forth the living creature after his kind, cattle, and creeping thing, and beast of the earth after his kind: and it was so. And God made the beast of the earth after his kind, and cattle after their kind, and everything that creped upon the earth after his kind: and God saw that it was good. And God said, **Let us make man in our image,** after our likeness: and let them have dominion over the fish of the sea, and over the fowl of the air, and over the cattle, and over all the Earth, and over every creeping thing that creped upon the Earth.

So God created man in his own image, in the image of God created he him; male and female created he them.

And God blessed them, and God said unto them, **Be fruitful, and multiply, and replenish the earth, and subdue it**: and have dominion over the fish of the sea, and over the fowl of the air, and over every living thing that moved upon the Earth. And God said, Behold, I have given you every herb bearing seed, which is upon the face of all the earth, and every tree, in the which is the fruit of a tree yielding seed; to you it shall be for meat. And to every beast of the earth, and to every fowl of the air, and to everything that creped upon the Earth, wherein there is life, I have given every green herb for meat: and it was so.

And **God saw every thing that he had made, and, behold, it was very good**.

And the evening and the morning were the sixth day.

Comment: God prepared the life conditions and created a human being to his image. He endowed this being with conscience. In a person we have a big conscience enrolled in a small matter. At this phase appears the second group of three-dimensional energy connected to the conscience. God entrusted with man his mission on Earth. His mission consists to subdue positively the surrounding World in order to get a positive energy. We find that this day corresponds to the phase of the apparition of conscience. After many years of positive evolution, it was the sixth phase of Earth's formation.

That is the phase of positive conscience and negative resources.

GOD'S REST (SEVENTH DAY)

Thus **the heavens and the earth were finished, and all the host of them.**

And on the seventh day God ended his work which he had made; and he rested on the seventh day from all his work which he had made. And **God blessed the seventh day, and sanctified it:** because that in it he had rested from all his work which God created and made.

These are the generations of the heavens and of the earth when they were created, in the day that the Lord God made the earth and the heavens.

Comment: That is the history of the creation and the evolution of Earth and any being in general. This is the phase of a human's activation and the launching of his intention and will. This is the phase of accomplishment.

We just solved the polemic existing between science and religion about the meaning of the creation of the world in seven days. One day means one phase and each phase can spread throughout billion years. The third chapter talks about the three phases of the negative.

CHAPTER 7

Application of The Triad Law To The Chemical Elements

Group→	1	2	3	4	5	6	7	8	9	10	11	12	13	14	15	16	17	18
↓Period					The Periodic Table of the Elements													
1	1 H																	2 He
2	3 Li	4 Be											5 B	6 C	7 N	8 O	9 F	10 Ne
3	11 Na	12 Mg											13 Al	14 Si	15 P	16 S	17 Cl	18 Ar
4	19 K	20 Ca	21 Sc	22 Ti	23 V	24 Cr	25 Mn	26 Fe	27 Co	28 Ni	29 Cu	30 Zn	31 Ga	32 Ge	33 As	34 Se	35 Br	36 Kr
5	37 Rb	38 Sr	39 Y	40 Zr	41 Nb	42 Mo	43 Tc	44 Ru	45 Rh	46 Pd	47 Ag	48 Cd	49 In	50 Sn	51 Sb	52 Te	53 I	54 Xe
6	55 Cs	56 Ba		72 Hf	73 Ta	74 W	75 Re	76 Os	77 Ir	78 Pt	79 Au	80 Hg	81 Tl	82 Pb	83 Bi	84 Po	85 At	86 Rn
7	87 Fr	88 Ra		104 Rf	105 Db	106 Sg	107 Bh	108 Hs	109 Mt	110 Ds	111 Rg	112 Cn	113 Nh	114 Fl	115 Mc	116 Lv	117 Ts	118 Og

Lanthanides	57 La	58 Ce	59 Pr	60 Nd	61 Pm	62 Sm	63 Eu	64 Gd	65 Tb	66 Dy	67 Ho	68 Er	69 Tm	70 Yb	71 Lu
Actinides	89 Ac	90 Th	91 Pa	92 U	93 Np	94 Pu	95 Am	96 Cm	97 Bk	98 Cf	99 Es	100 Fm	101 Md	102 No	103 Lr

After studying our solar system in its static and dynamic plans, we will pass to the atomic world. We will make our studies on their static and dynamic plans to prove the existence and the smooth working of the triad's law in this relatively small world. Mendeleev made this periodic table or chart in 1868. He found out that minerals when arranged according to the magnitude of their increasing atomic weights, present a visible periodicity of their properties.

Later after the discovery of the electronic structures, Bohr made a classification based on the analogy of electronic structures of the neuter atoms. Mendeleev was deeply convinced that he had just discovered a basic law of the nature (the triad law).

While observing this table, we will remark the following points:

1. Horizontally we have 7 rows or periods.
2. Vertically we have 7 groups subdivided into 7 sub-groups A and 7 sub-groups B. We also have the group Zero, or group of rare gases, or inert gasses that belongs to another structure.
3. There are three other groups of 4 elements each between the subgroup A and subgroup B. These groups are called groups of triad. They correspond to the three groups of the negative.

Observing the first group of the table, we note that the sub-group (B) is made of the most valued minerals on Earth. This is the subgroup of Cu, Ag, Au- (Copper, Silver, and Gold). These three minerals constitute respectively the bronze, silver, and gold medals of Olympic Games. We express our material and financial wealth through these metals. Through them or their equivalent, we buy knowledge and techniques. For this reason we always look for them or for things that are equivalent to them such as money.

Finally, we can state that to each group of the minerals corresponds a planet, a state of soul, a sign, and a phase of life.

GROUP	1	2	3	4	5
PLANET	Earth	Mars	Mercury	Jupiter	Venus

GROUP	6	7	8	9	10
PLANET	Saturn	Sun	Neptune	Uranus	Pluto

CHAPTER 8

Significance Of The Ten Universal Numbers

In this part we use the triad's law to enumerate some appearances of the numbers going from 1 to 10 under different forms.

We are going just to show that a number expresses not only a quantitative value, but also a qualitative value. Each number corresponds to a state of soul on the static plan. It corresponds to a phase of a process, to a step of an evolution on the dynamic plan. It corresponds to a level expressing a quality, to a day of the week on the religious plan. It corresponds to a planet in astrology, and to a group of the periodic table in chemistry.

Let's enumerate these 10 numbers under different implications.

The number ONE represents the birth of a being, and the appearance of his intention and will.

It corresponds to the first phase of an action, to the first step of an evolution.

In human life, 1 corresponds to the birth and the apparition of the intention and will.

In action, it corresponds to the positive intention and will.

In religion, it marks the first day of the week Monday.

In astrology, Monday represents the moon and the planet Earth. Earth is the sphere of positive will.

In chemistry, it corresponds to the first group of the periodic table of the elements.

In social evolution of humanity, it corresponds to the phase of positive will.

The number TWO shows the orientation of this will by a being's intention towards the acquisition of physical possession.

It corresponds to the second phase of an action, to the second step of an evolution.

In human life, 2 corresponds to the phase of his physical growth.

In action, it corresponds to the positive activity.

In religion, it marks the second day of the week Tuesday.

In astrology, Tuesday represents the planet Mars. Mars is the sphere of the positive activity.

In chemistry, it corresponds to the second group of the periodic table of the elements.

In social evolution of humanity, it corresponds to the phase of positive activity.

The number THREE represents the necessary use of the will and possession of a being towards the acquisition of knowledge.

It corresponds to the third phase of an action, to the third step of an evolution.

In human life, 3 corresponds to the phase of his intellectual formation.

In action, it corresponds to the phase of the positive knowledge.

In religion, it marks the third day of the week Wednesday.

In astrology, Wednesday represents the planet mercury. Mercury is the sphere of the positive knowledge.

In chemistry, it corresponds to the third group of the periodic table of the elements.

In social evolution of humanity it corresponds to the phase of the positive knowledge.

The number FOUR represents the apparition and the formation of the power of a being.

It corresponds to the fourth phase of an action, to the fourth step of an evolution.

In human life, 4 corresponds to the phase of his enfranchisement.

In action, it corresponds to the phase of the positive power.

In religion, it marks the fourth day of the week Thursday.

In astrology, Thursday represents the planet Jupiter and its satellites. Jupiter is the sphere of the positive power.

In chemistry, it corresponds to the fourth group of the periodic table.

In social evolution of humanity it corresponds to the phase of positive power.

The number FIVE represents the being's acquisition of material wealth through production.

It corresponds to the fifth phase of an action, to the fifth step of an evolution.

In human life, 5 corresponds to the phase of obtaining material and financial wealth.

In action, it corresponds to the phase of the positive possession.

In religion, it marks the fifth day of the week Friday.

In astrology, Friday represents the planet Venus. Venus is the sphere of positive possession.

In chemistry, it corresponds to the fifth group of the Periodical table.

In social evolution of humanity it corresponds to the phase of the positive possession or phase of high productivity.

The number SIX represents the handling of the being's intention with knowledge.

It corresponds to the sixth phase of an action, to the sixth step of an evolution.

In human's, 6 corresponds to the phase of positive conscience or wisdom.

In action, it corresponds to the phase of positive conscience.

In religion, it corresponds to the sixth day of the week: Saturday.

In astrology, Saturday represents the planet Saturn. Saturn is the sphere of the positive conscience.

In chemistry, it corresponds to the sixth group of the periodic table of the elements.

In social evolution of humanity, it corresponds to the phase of positive conscience or phase of great social transformation.

The number SEVEN represents the accomplishment of a being.

It corresponds to the seventh phase of an action, to the seventh step of an evolution.

In human's life, 7 corresponds to the phase of accomplishment, happiness and freedom.

In action, it corresponds to the phase of freedom and of happiness.

In religion, it corresponds to the seventh day of the week: Sunday.

In astrology, Sunday represents the Sun. Sun is the planet of beauty and perfect harmony.

In chemistry, it corresponds to the seventh group of the periodic table of the elements.

In social evolution of humanity, it corresponds to the phase of freedom and happiness.

The number EIGHT represents the submission of the being to another one more powerful and constraining. The submissive being becomes inert, passive and obeys unconditionally to the desire of the constraining one.

It corresponds to the eighth phase of an action, to the eighth step of an evolution or to the first phase of a negative evolution.

In human life, 8 corresponds to the phase of submission.

In religion, it does not have a day it is part of the night.

In astrology, this phase of resignation, submission and inertia corresponds to the planet Neptune. Neptune is the sphere of dreams, illusion, and submission.

In the social evolution of humanity, it corresponds to the phase of submission of a people to dictatorships.

The number NINE represents the ephemeral sensation of the oppressed being to become free.

This delivered oppressed being for a limited time feels happy and forgets his tortures and miseries.

It corresponds to the ninth phase of an action, to the ninth step of an evolution or to the second step of a negative evolution.

In human life, it corresponds to the phase of depravity, false happiness and torture.

In religion, it corresponds also to the night.

In astrology, this depravity and dependent phase corresponds to the planet Uranus. Uranus is the sphere of depravity and false happiness.

In social evolution of humanity, it corresponds to the phase of depravity.

The number TEN represents the determination of a being to use all his force to break indefinitely and radically with the structures of a constraining power.

It corresponds to the tenth phase of an action, to the tenth step of an evolution and to the third step of a negative evolution.

In human life, 10 corresponds to the exit of his soul to another sphere by force.

In religion, it represents human' death but does not have any day.

In astrology, this phase corresponds to the planet Pluto. Pluto is the sphere of shock, revolt, suicide, war, adventure, revolution or sometime degradation.

In social evolution of humanity, it corresponds to the phase of shock, revolt and revolution or degradation.

CHAPTER 9

The Great Star Of Life

Let's return to the triad which is based on the connection of the ends of the axes of the three one-dimensional components. (Intention, Knowledge and Resources- Figure on the left side)

Let's compare this system to the one which is based on the connection of the ends of the axes of the three two-dimensional components. (Conscience Activity and Power– Figure on the right side).

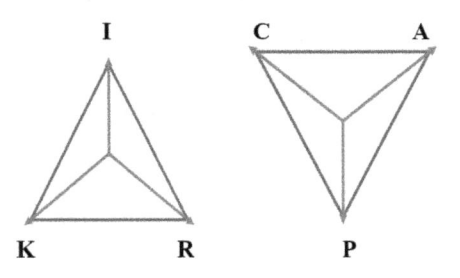

By assembling these two systems and removing their axes of coordinates, we obtain a figure that we call the STAR OF LIFE or the GREAT STAR

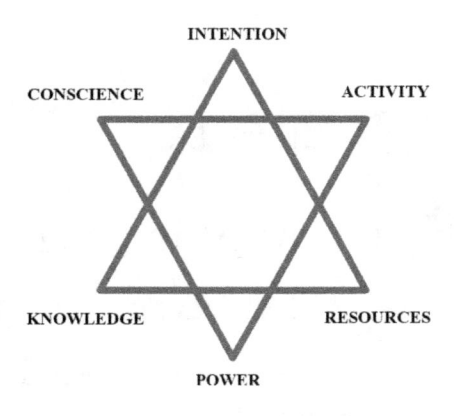

```
                    INTENTION
        CONSCIENCE            ACTIVITY




        KNOWLEDGE             RESOURCES
                    POWER
```

THIS STAR LOOKS EXACTLY LIKE

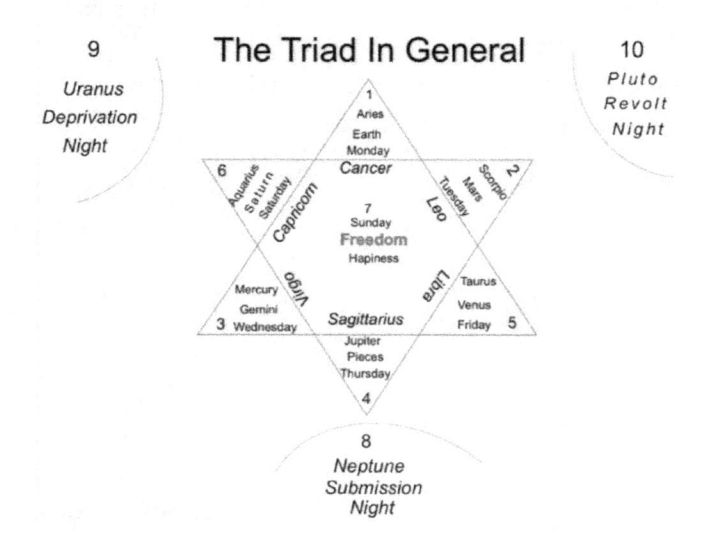

9 **The Triad In General** **10**

Uranus — *Pluto*
Deprivation — *Revolt*
Night — *Night*

```
              1
           Aries
           Earth
           Monday
    6     Cancer        2
  Aquarius              Scorpio
  Saturn   Tuesday      Mars
  Saturday Leo
  Capricorn
           7
           Sunday
           Freedom
           Hapiness
                 Libra
  Mercury        Taurus
  Gemini         Venus
 3 Wednesday Sagittarius Friday 5
           Jupiter
           Pieces
           Thursday
              4
```

8
Neptune
Submission
Night

This Star looks also like what some people call Star of David, Seal of Solomon etc.

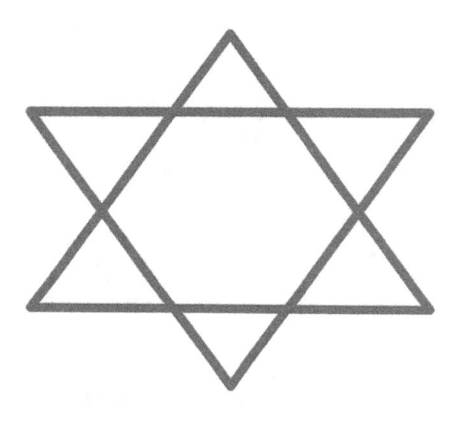

By replacing the states of soul by their planets, we get the Triad applied to the Solar System.

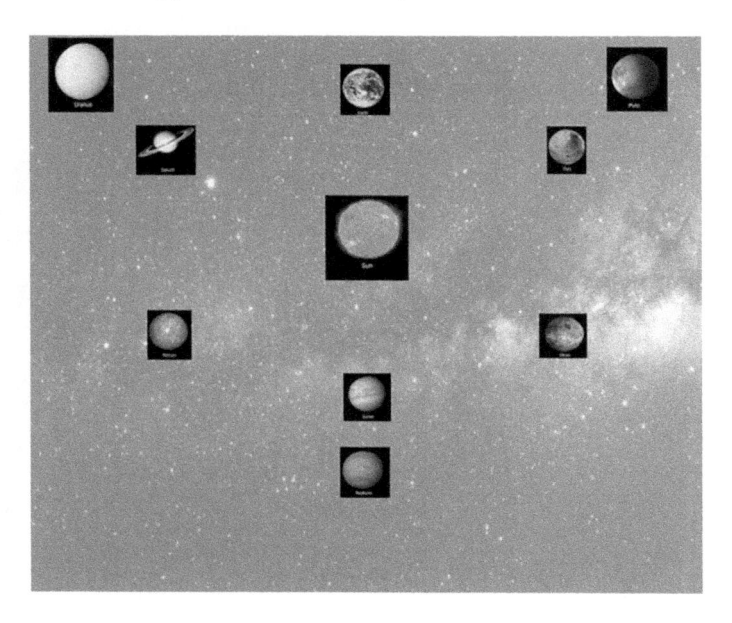

By rotating the system around its axis.
We get the following Figures.

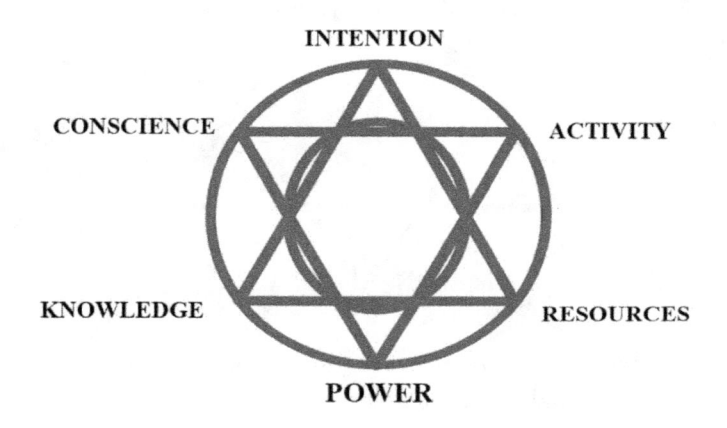

```
              INTENTION

CONSCIENCE              ACTIVITY



KNOWLEDGE               RESOURCES

               POWER
```

It may also be presented in this form

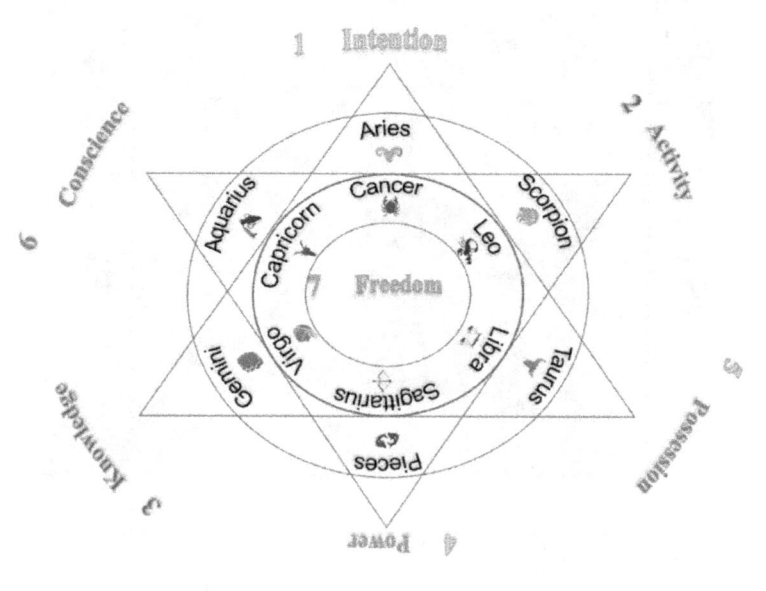

```
1 Intention
2 Activity
3 Knowledge
4 Power
5 Possession
6 Conscience

Aries, Cancer, Scorpion, Leo, Libra, Taurus, Sagittarius, Pisces, Gemini, Virgo, Capricorn, Aquarius

7 Freedom
```

Let's bring back the 3 parts of the negative and turn the system to the right for 60 degrees around its axis.

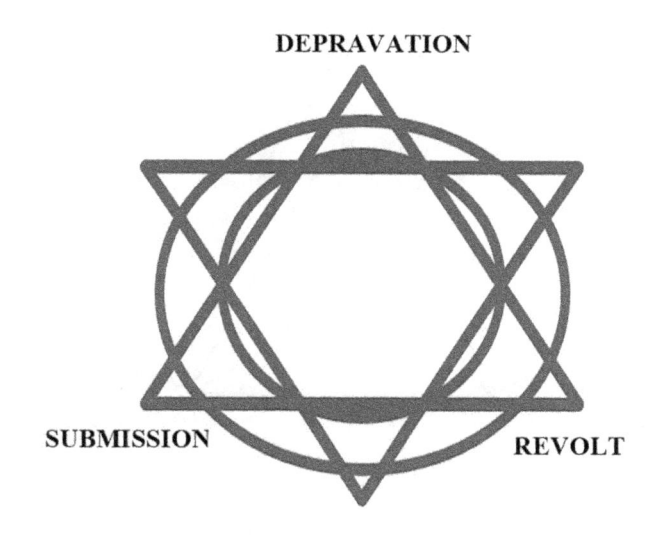

DEPRAVATION

SUBMISSION **REVOLT**

This figure resembles to what we call Circles of Mystery or Crop Circles (Figure on the right)

TRIAD IN GENERAL **CIRCLES OF MYSTERY**

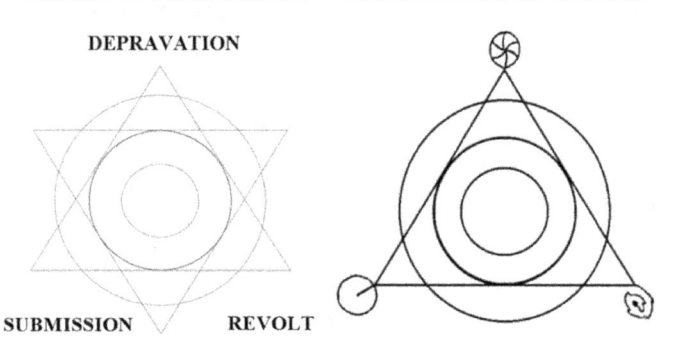

DEPRAVATION

SUBMISSION **REVOLT**

THE CIRCLES OF MYSTERY
(CROP-CIRCLES)

These mysterious circles appeared during the last 30 years in more than twenty countries including the USA, Canada and Australia. There were several versions of explanation of their origins.

The first explanation asserts that these circles were formed by a polarization of air currents. The second theory asserts that they were formed by an interaction of mysterious forces. The third explanation states that spiritual forces constructed these circles. The fourth one asserts that these circles are message carriers and were left by aliens when they visited our planet. The last explanation is made by two English painters who claim to be the builders of these circles. Without entering in details let's focus on the three external circles.

Observing these 3 circles from the left to the right, it can be noted:

The first circle is a circle held by just one arm. This occurs when an iron arm holds the being solidly. This is the phase of a submission of a being to dictatorship.

The second circle has one center held by several twisted forces. This occurs when the being is submitted to the forces of torsion. This is a sphere held by several groups of bad consciences. The forces of the center of this circle want to return the circle towards the left side while the forces of the periphery want to turn the circle towards the right. This is the phase of torture and depravity.

The third circle corresponds to a sphere of rupture of all arms and the apparition of a new center. This new center marks the advent of a new life (Trans-life). This is the sphere of the shock and revolution or sometimes degradation.

This last sphere is made of 7 sub-phases or 7 breaking points. That means this phase of shock like any other phases divide itself in 7 successive and coherent sub phases.

We see finally that these circles are only a new representation of the triad's law. The only difference is on the choice of the components of the system of coordinates. Let's recognize that this form of representation is the most descriptive. The next figure shows the full picture. It may also be presented in this form.

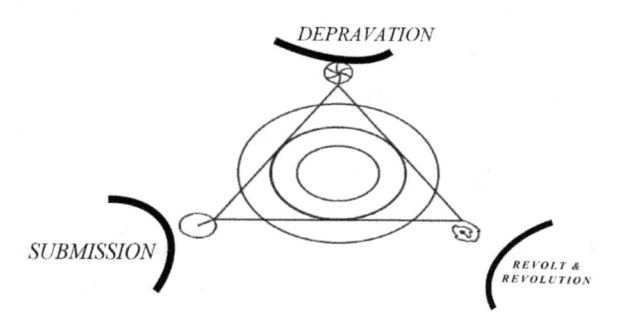

CHAPTER 10

Hermes' Vision

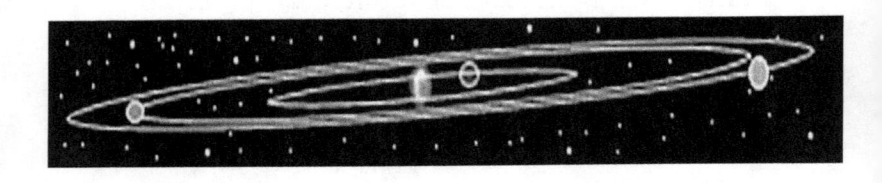

In this part we will talk about the most important points of Hermes Vision.

This vision is a dream in which Hermes received a revelation from his God Osiris about the path of souls after death and the signs of planets (Some parts will be followed by comments based on triad law). Each comment starts with the word "Comment".

The Vision of Hermes is found at the beginning of his books, Trismegistus, under the name of "Pomanders". Hermes (is a Greco- Egyptian personage connected to many mystical and philosophical books). The ancient Egyptian traditions have come down to us only in a slightly changed Alexandrian form.

Here is the vision

One day, Hermes, after reflecting on the origin of things, fell asleep. A dull torpor took possession of his body; but in proportion as the latter grew be numbered, his spirit ascended into space. Then an immense being, of indeterminate form, seemed to call him by name. "Who are you?" said the terrified Hermes. "I am Osiris, the sovereign Intelligence who is able to unveil all things. What do you desire?" "Since things are so," said Hermes, "grant that I may see the light of the worlds; the path of souls from which man comes and to which he returns." "Be it done according to your desire. " Hermes became heavier than a stone and fell through space like a meteorite. Finally he reached the summit of a mountain. It was night, the earth was gloomy and deserted, and his limbs seemed as heavy as iron. "Raise your eyes and look!" said the voice of Osiris. Then Hermes saw a wonderful sight.

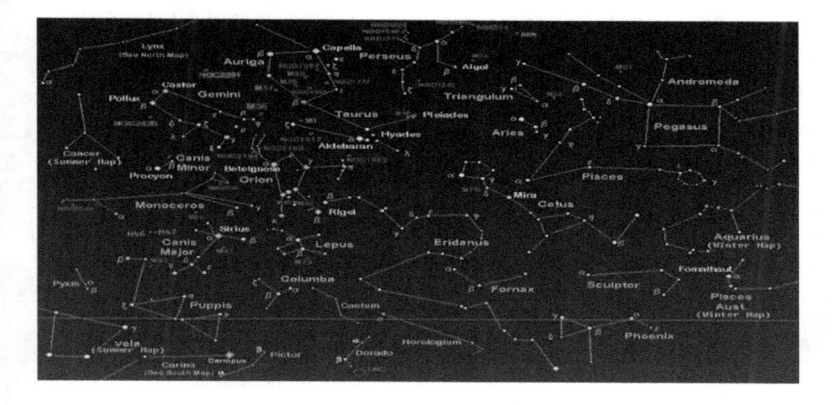

The starry heavens, stretching through infinite space, enveloped him with seven luminous spheres. In one glance, Hermes saw the seven heavens stretching above his head, tier upon tier, like seven transparent and concentric globes, and the sidereal center of which he now occupied. The Milky Way formed the girdle of the last.

In each sphere there rolled a planet accompanied by a genius of different form, sign and light. Whilst Hermes, dazzled by the sight, was contemplating their wide-spread efflorescence and majestic movements, the voice said to him: "Look, listen, and understand. You see the seven spheres of all life. Through them is accomplished the fall and ascent of souls. The seven genii are the seven rays of the word-light. Each of them commands one sphere of the spirit, one phase of the life of souls. The one nearest to you is the Genius of the Moon, with his disquieting smile and crown of silver sickle. He presides over births and deaths, sets free souls from bodies and draws them into his ray.

Comment: At birth any being (the Moon as Earth's satellite) is endowed with a positive will and a negative Power.

Above him, pale Mercury points out the path to ascending or descending souls with his caduceus which contains knowledge.

Comment: Mercury is the sphere of the positive knowledge and the negative activity.

Higher still, shining Venus holds the mirror of love, in which souls forget and recognize them in turn.

Comment: Venus is the sphere of forgetfulness; the planet of the negative conscience, and positive possession.

Above her, the Genius of the Sun raises the triumphal torch of eternal beauty.

Comment: The Sun is in the solar system, but it belongs to another structure. It corresponds to the accomplishment.

At a yet loftier height, Mars brandishes the sword of justice.

Comment: Mars is a sphere of activity led with artfulness. Mars is the planet of the positive activity and the negative knowledge.

Enthroned on the azure sphere, Jupiter holds the specter of supreme power, which is divine intelligence.

Comment: Jupiter is the sphere of positive power and negative intention.

At the boundaries of the world, beneath the signs of the Zodiac, Saturn bears the globe of universal wisdom.

Comment: Saturn is a sphere of positive conscience and negative possession.

"I see," said Hermes, "the seven regions which comprise the visible and the invisible world; I see the seven rays of the word-light, of the one God who traverses them and governs them by these rays. Strengthen therefore your soul, O Hermes! Calm your darkened mind by contemplating these distant flights of souls which mount the seven spheres and are scattered about therein like sheaves of sparks. You also can follow them, but a strong will it needs to rise.

Comment: Earth is the planet of positive will and negative power.

The vision of Hermes resembles the starry heaven, whose unfathomable depths are strewn with constellations.

For the sage it is boundless space in which worlds revolve, with their wonderful rhythms and cadences.

This vision contains the eternal numbers, the magic keys (Days or Planets) and the evocating signs (States of Soul).

NUMBER	*DAY*	*PLANET*	*STATE OF SOUL*
1	Monday	Moon-Earth	Positive intention
2	Tuesday	Mars	Positive Activity
3	Wednesday	Mercury	Positive Knowledge
4	Thursday	Jupiter	Positive Power
5	Friday	Venus	Positive Possession
6	Saturday	Saturn	Positive Conscience
7	Sunday	Sun	Accomplishment
8	Night	Neptune	Submission

9	Night	Uranus	Depravation
10	Night	Pluto	Revolt

For where everything ends, everything eternally begins; and the seven spheres say together: "Beauty! (Accomplishment), Wisdom! (Conscience), Love! (Possession), Splendor! (Power), Knowledge! (Knowledge), Justice! (Activity), Immortality! (Intention and Will)"

The seven spheres attached to the seven planets symbolize seven principles, seven different states of matter and spirit, seven different worlds which each man and each humanity are forced to pass through in their evolution across a solar system.

The seven genii or the seven cosmogonist Gods signify the superior, directing spirits of all spheres, the off-spring of inevitable evolution.

The seven genii of the vision of Hermes are the seven colors of the rainbow, the seven notes of the scale, the seven groups and the seven periods of chemical elements, the seven heavens, the seven days of a week, the seven chakras, the seven states of soul etc. It also manifests itself in the constitution of man, which is triple in essence, but sevenfold in its evolution.

That is what according to the hierophant saw the antique HERMES and what his successors reported to us.

BIBLIOGRAPHIE

1. The mystery of the Conscience and the Power of the Negative New generation Publishing. St. Louis, MO. 63130. USA, 2001. ISBN: 09648181-40

2. Les Grands Initiés. Edouard Schuré. Librairy Academique, PERRIN 1960 France.

3. La philosophie comme debats entre les textes. José Medina, Claude Morali, André Senik. Edition N 7240. Dépot légal 1987.

4. Chimie minérale. Boris Nékrassov. Editions MIR. Moscou 1987 Russia.

5. Holly Bible. The International Gideon. 29 Road Lebanon. Tennessee Nashville, 1974.

6. The astrological Tool. Evers Joan Mc 1989. Minnesota USA

All rights reserved. No part of this book may be reproduced, stored in retrieval systems, or transmitted in any form by any means, including mechanical electronics, without written permission from the author, except by a reviewer who may quote brief passages in a review.

Printed in the USA
CPSIA information can be obtained
at www.ICGtesting.com
CBHW051738051024
15371CB00042B/1120

9 781962 868679